Mary Callery   Sculpture

Mary Callery   Sculpture

Distributed by Wittenborn and Company

1018 Madison Avenue, New York 21, New York

Introduction translated from the English by G. P. La Vieille

Printed in Germany, 1961

A work of sculpture is an object in space. At least it begins by being simply that, and can go on to become many other things, such as a distillation of the artist's personality, or more importantly an embodied idea. But the swift-moving twentieth century has modified this accepted definition to the extent that a work of sculpture to-day might well be called an object involved with space.

Perhaps the change set in with the later works of Rodin when it seemed as if his cursorily modelled forms were trying to hurl themselves into violent movement, and as tracer bullets of swirling motion come to a new life. The young Roumanian, however, who began to study with Rodin in 1906 found another solution. Far from turning his back on the traditional forms of sculpture Brancusi sought out their inmost, their abstract being. And it is not extravagant to say that all things moving swiftly through the air or sea, or on land to-day speed in the shapes Brancusi had designed for them as early as 1910. If Rodin dissolved mass into motion, Brancusi gave motion itself an abiding shape.

Between these sculptural poles the best modern sculptors have taken their individual ways to find their personal styles, sometimes veering more towards the one than the other, sometimes combining the virtues of both extremes. None has done so more skilfully, possibly no one has done it as skilfully as Mary Callery. Nor has anyone more surely fused taste and intelligence to achieve a highly personal expression.

Christian Zervos in 1950 came close to defining her particular quality - "In Mary Callery's studies of acrobats she chooses those attitudes in which all is calculated precision: where every breach of discipline must be thwarted and adjusted, every liberty at once subjected to the laws of balance. That which is difficult must seem easy, that which is heavy must seem light, the unstable and the temporary must appear set and immutable. This is the extraordinary and strange exploit that both the artist and the acrobat undertake. They seem to go their way at random, happen what may, but both are exposed to the danger of the slightest false step; and for artist and acrobat alike everything depends on the success of a concept carefully and slowly worked out, governed by a rigorous logic."

Mary Callery of New York and Paris, as she might be identified in this international age, was born in New York in 1903 and began her study of sculpture here. From 1930 to 1940 she worked in France, powerfully stimulated by close friendship with Picasso and the vigorous intellectual climate of Paris. She returned to New York in 1940 and presented her first American exhibition at that shrine of perceptive modernism, the Curt Valentin Gallery, then the Buchholz Gallery. Succeeding exhibitions there in 1944, 1947, 1950, 1952 and 1955 showed how certainly she had found her path and with what confidence she was journeying on it. It was not a straight-edged highway, but curved, endlessly like the lithe lines of her sculptured figures, opening new vistas at every turn.

In 1955 the artist herself said, "What should a sculpture be? Above all it must be plastic. But to be a work of art, to me, it must have its emotional life. One must like the thing, be attracted to it, or even be repulsed. It must work on you. Only then does it become living. That was for me the hardest thing to learn. I was slow, I am slow, even now I feel that the dawn is only breaking before my clearing vision."

This is characteristic but undue modesty, since the 1944 exhibition showed a high percentage of complete arrivals, among them the monumental *Horse* of 1942, with its evocation of archaic Greece. *Reclining Figure, Musician* and *Dancers* are already attenuated, weaving in and out with the fluent grace which is Mary Callery's autograph. *Constellation* is equally successful in its more rigid geometric stress.

The theme of slender, almost linear, interweaving figures was brilliantly developed in the following years. Light enough to fly or float, they literally do so in *Composition on Glass,* first seen in the 1947 exhibition. Also present then were such distinguished variations on the theme as *Acrobats* of 1945, *Amity* of 1947 and *The Curve* of the same year. But in spite of this thematic unity Mary Callery refused to repeat a formula; *Song of the Desert's* subtle modelling derives from organic natural shapes and her portraits grew in authority. Not many leading sculptors of the day are either able or willing to range from schematic abstractions, suggested by nature perhaps but resolutely opposed to imitating the appearances of nature, to literal portrait likenesses. Lipchitz is a notable exception and Mary Callery finds portrait sculpture both refreshing and enriching. She says, "In the matter of my portraits: it is a different fascination to work from real life. The works done without a model help unendingly when one is again face to face with nature. All the things one has found poor when working alone suddenly become clear when one has the opportunity again to work from actuality. This experience with the actual has in its turn a wonderful new and healthy effect on more objective work. The change from nature to one's own imagination and vice versa is continually enriching."

Mary Callery also felt that lack of color in modern sculpture was an unnecessary impoverishment. After all the Greeks and Egyptians painted their carvings boldly and a Gothic cathedral was a joyful noise of color. So she collaborated through the nineteen-forties with no less a painter than Fernand Leger against whose patterned backgrounds of primary colors her sinuous figures weave their arabesques. The architectural possibilities of this innovation were striking and insufficiently exploited by the architectural fraternity, though in 1953 Mary Callery produced *The Birds, Constellation I* and *Constellation II* for the Aluminum Company of America's headquarters building in Pittsburgh. *The Fables of La Fontaine* embellished the severely modern structure of Public School Number 34 on East Twelfth Street in 1954, and in 1955 *Acrobats, Monument* rose against the façade of Wingate Public School in Brooklyn.

Both the genuinely playful *Fables,* designed for school children to climb and crawl through - fully as efficient as the usual playground jungle gym and infinitely more decorative - and *Acrobats* are a departure from the slightly-modelled lines of Mary Callery's more familiar figures. *Acrobats* suggests scrap-metal in its angularity while the *Fables* recalls I-beams and the U-section of unistrut. The late forties and early fifties saw many other variations from the Callery norm: *Fish in Reeds* of 1948 uses the full silhouette of its subjects; *The Young Diana I* of 1953 and the painted aluminum of *Three Birds in Flight* of the same year are successful experiments, while *The Flirt* of 1957 combines many of these elements in its engaging portrait of a French poodle.

Three highly frog-like *Frogs* of 1956, one in bronze, one in steel and the third in painted steel, are a return to sophisticated natural modelling. But *The Maze No. 4* and *Composition with Tendrils* both of 1957 are almost entirely abstract as is the ingeniously conceived *Fountain* of 1958, except that it might equally well be called a portrait of flowing water. This ability to make a synthesis of her experiments and summon all her resources to each new work is a mark of Mary Callery's artistic maturity. So too is her willingness, and ability, to try for new solutions. And throughout her career the growing authority of her style, with its sure wit and grace, has been warmed by an implicit womanly strength.

Philip R. Adams

Une sculpture est un objet dans l'espace. Du moins c'est ce qu' elle est d'abord, et elle peut par la suite devenir beaucoup d'autres choses, telles que: une quintessence de la personnalité de l'artiste, ou mieux encore une idée qui a pris corps. Mais le siècle d'évolution rapide qu'est le vingtième siècle a modifié cette définition reconnue, au point qu'une sculpture aujourd'hui pourrait justement se dénommer un objet impliqué dans l'espace.

Peut-être ce changement s'est-il introduit avec les dernières oeuvres de Rodin quand il sembla que ses formes rapidement modelées cherchaient à se mettre brutalement en branle, pareilles à des balles traceuses au mouvement tourbillonnant qui auraient pris vie. Cependant le jeune Roumain qui commença à étudier avec Rodin à Paris en 1906 trouva une autre solution.

Loin de tourner le dos aux formes traditionnelles de la sculpture Brancusi rechercha leur être profond et abstrait. Et il n'est pas exagéré de dire que toutes les choses qui se meuvent rapidement dans les airs ou la mer, ou sur terre aujourd'hui filent sous les formes que Brancusi avait conçues pour elles dès 1910. Si Rodin a résolu la masse en mouvement, Brancusi a donné au mouvement même une forme permanente.

Entre ces deux pôles de la sculpture les meilleurs sculpteurs modernes ont pris des chemins individuels pour trouver leur style personnel, parfois inclinant plus vers l'un que vers l'autre, parfois combinant les vertus des deux extrêmes. Aucun ne l'a fait plus, ou peut-être aussi, habilement que Mary Callery. Aucun non plus n'a fusionné avec plus d'assurance le goût et l'intelligence pour atteindre à une expression hautement personnelle.

Christian Zervos en 1950 a serré de près sa qualité propre: "Des mouvements des acrobates, Callery retient ceux où tout est calculé, où chaque infraction à la discipline se déjoue et se rajuste, où toute liberté est aussitôt contrainte par les exigences de l'équilibre à réaliser, où la difficulté doit se transformer en aisance et la pesanteur en légèreté, où l'instable et le provisoire doivent paraître fixes et comme définitifs.

C'est là le tour extraordinaire et la singulière gageure tenue par l'acrobate et l'artiste qui s'en inspire. Tous deux ont l'air d'aller droit devant eux à l'aventure et au petit bonheur de la rencontre, alors qu'ils courent l'extrême péril du moindre faux mouvement et que tout dépend pour l'un et l'autre de la réussite d'une figure longuement préparée, dominée par une logique rigoureuse."

Mary Callery de New-York et de Paris, ainsi qu'on pourrait la nommer en ce siècle international, est née à New-York en 1903 et c'est là qu'elle a commencé à étudier la sculpture. De 1930 à 1940 elle a travaillé en France, puissamment stimulée par une amitié étroite avec Picasso et le climat intellectuel vigoureux de Paris. Elle est retournée à New-York en 1940 et a présenté sa première exposition américaine dans ce sanctuaire du modernisme "perceptif", la Galerie Curt Valentin, en ce moment la Galerie Buchholz. Des expositions successives en 1944, 1947, 1950, 1952 et 1955 ont révélé avec quelle certitude elle avait trouvé sa voie et avec quelle confiance elle s'y avançait. Ce n'était pas une grande route rectiligne, mais sinueuse à l'infini comme les souples lignes de ses figures sculptées, ouvrant de nouvelles perspectives à chaque détour.

En 1955 l'artiste a dit elle-même: "Que devrait être une sculpture? Avant tout elle doit être plastique. Mais pour être une oeuvre d'art, pour moi, il faut qu'elle ait sa vie émotive. Il faut qu'on l'aime, qu'on soit attiré par elle, ou même repoussé. Elle doit agir sur nous. Alors seulement elle devient vivante. C'est ce qui m'a été le plus difficile à apprendre. J'ai été lente, je suis lente, même maintenant je sens que l'aube se lève seulement à ma vue qui s'éclaire."

C'est caractéristique, mais d'une modestie exagérée, puisque l'exposition de 1944 a montré un pourcentage élevé d'oeuvres achevées, parmi lesquelles le *Cheval* monumental de 1942 avec son évocation de la Grèce archaïque. *Figure Étendue*, *Musicien* et *Danseurs* sont déjà atténués, car s'y insinue la grâce aisée qui est la signature de Mary Callery. *Constellation* est également une réussite avec son accent géométrique plus rigide.

Le thème des figures élancées, presque linéaires, qui s'enchevêtrent a été brillamment développé dans les années suivantes. Assez légères pour voler ou flotter, elles le font littéralement dans *Composition sur Verre*, que l'on vit pour la première fois à l'exposition de 1947. Figuraient aussi alors des variations sur ce thème aussi remarquables que les *Acrobates* de 1945, l'*Amitié* de 1947 et la *Courbe* de la même année. Mais en dépit de cette unité de thème Mary Callery a refusé de répéter une formule; le modelé subtil de *Chant du Désert* dérive de formes naturelles organiques et ses portraits ont gagné en autorité.

Il n'y a pas beaucoup de sculpteurs de poids aujourd'hui qui soient ou capables ou désireux d'étendre leur registre d'abstractions schématiques, suggérées par la nature peut-être mais se refusant catégoriquement à imiter les apparences de la nature, jusqu'aux ressemblances littérales du portrait. Lipchitz est une exception notable et Mary Callery trouve que le portrait sculpté est à la fois délassant et enrichissant. Elle dit: "Pour ce qui est de mes portraits: c'est un charme différent que de travailler d'après la vie réelle. Les oeuvres faites sans modèles aident infiniment quand on est à nouveau face à face avec la nature. Toutes les choses qu'on a trouvées médiocres quand on travaillait seul tout à coup deviennent claires quand on a l'occasion de retravailler d'après la réalité. Cette expérience avec le réel à son tour a un nouvel effet merveilleux et salutaire sur une oeuvre plus objective. Le passage de la nature à son imagination et vice versa est un enrichissement perpétuel."

Mary Callery a senti aussi que le manque de couleur dans la sculpture moderne a été un appauvrissement inutile. Après tout les Grecs et les Egyptiens peignaient leurs sculptures hardiment et une cathédrale gothique était un joyeux concert de couleurs. Aussi a-t-elle collaboré entre 1940 et 1950 avec un peintre, non des moindres, Fernand Léger; et c'est sur les motifs de fond aux couleurs primaires de ce dernier que ses figures sinueuses tissent leurs arabesques. Les possibilités architecturales de cette innovation furent frappantes et insuffisamment exploitées par la confrérie des architectes, quoique en 1953 Mary Callery produisit les *Oiseaux, Constellation I* et *Constellation II* pour les bâtiments du Siége Social de la Compagnie de l'Aluminium (l'Alcoa Building) à Pittsburgh. Les *Fables de La Fontaine* embellirent la structure sévèrement moderne du Lycée 34 dans la 12ème Rue à New-York en 1954, et en 1955 *Acrobates, Monument* se dressèrent sur la façade du Lycée Wingate à Brooklyn.

Comme les *Fables* amusantes, conçues pour que des écoliers y grimpent ou y rampent (tout aussi efficaces que les appareils du gymnase habituel et infiniment plus décoratives) les *Acrobates* s'écartent des lignes au modelé léger des figures plus familières de Mary Callery. Le groupe des *Acrobates* suggère le feuillard par ce qu'il a d'angulaire tandis que les *Fables* rappellent le fer en double T et la section des poutres en fer à U. Aux alentours de 1950 parurent beaucoup d'autres variations de la norme Callery: *Poissons dans les Roseaux* de 1948 recourt à la pleine silhouette de ses sujets; la *Jeune Diane I* de 1953 et l'aluminium peint de *Trois Oiseaux en Vol* de la même année sont des tentatives heureuses, tandis que *Flirt* de 1957 combine nombre de ces éléments dans son portrait attrayant d'un caniche français.

Trois Grenouilles vraiment réalistes de 1956, une en bronze, une en acier et la troisième en acier peint, sont un retour au naturalisme recherché. Mais *Labyrinthe n° 4* et *Composition aux Vrilles* tous deux de 1957 sont presque entièrement abstraits comme l'est le *Jet d'Eau* ingénieux de conception de 1958, sauf qu'on pourrait également bien l'intituler Représentation d'eau courante.

Cette aptitude à faire une synthèse de ses expériences et à mettre en oeuvre toutes ses ressources pour chaque oeuvre nouvelle est une marque de la maturité artistique de Mary Callery. De même encore son désir, et sa capacité, d'essayer de nouvelles solutions. Et tout au long de sa carrière l'autorité croissante de son style, à la grâce et à l'esprit sûrs, a été chauffée par une vigueur féminine implicite.

Philip R. Adams

1

Musician - 1942 - Bronze - 12 ³/₄″ high

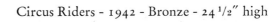
Circus Riders - 1942 - Bronze - 24 1/2″ high

Horse - 1942 - Bronze - 47 1/2″ high ▷

Plant - 1942 - Bronze - 9 1/4″ long

2

Reclining Figure (¹/₄ scale) - 1942 - Bronze - 2 ¹/₂′ long

Reclining Figure - 1944 - Bronze - 105″ long

Reclining Figure

The Tree - 1943
Bronze - 41″ high

Dancers - 1944 - Bronze - 48″ high

Branches - 1943 - Bronze - 23 ¹/₂″ x 36″

Constellation - 1944 - Plaster - 48″ high

Acrobats - 1945 - Bronze
44″ x 20″ x 24″

Song of the Desert - 1945 - Bronze - 25″ high

Five Acrobats - 1945 - Bronze - 19″ high ▷

Small Ballet - 1944 - Bronze - 12″ x 6¹/₂″

10

Seated Ballet - 1946 - Bronze - 64″ x 46″ ▷

Study for Seated Ballet - 1945 - Bronze
19³/₄″ x 13¹/₂″

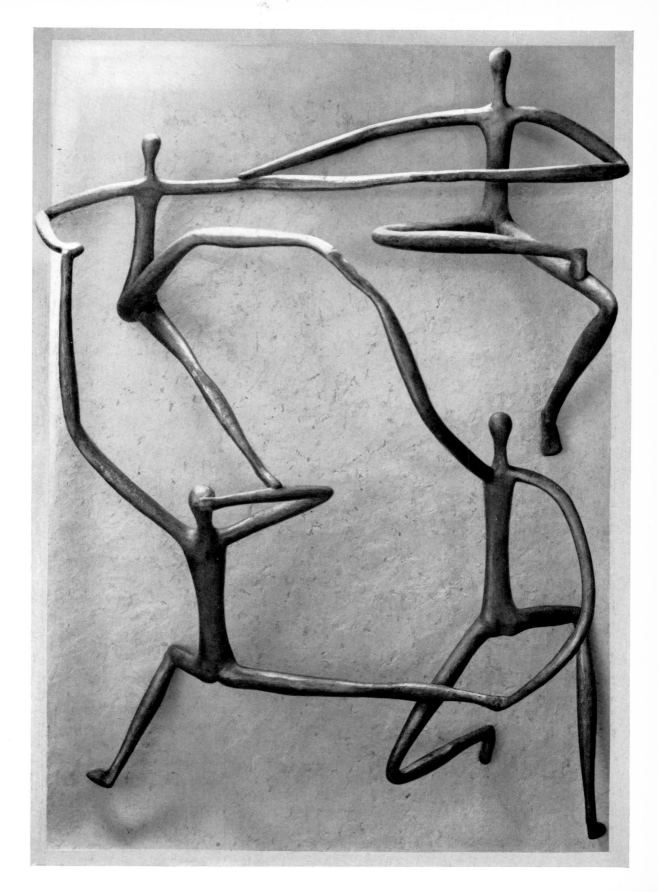

Head of a Girl - 1942 - Bronze - 11″ high ▷

Portrait of Harry Mathews - 1942 - Bronze - 12″ high

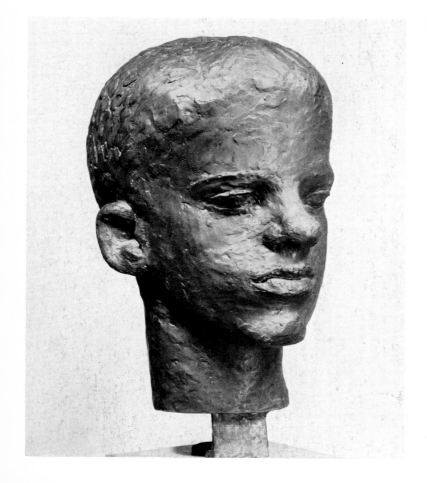

Portrait of Sally - 1945 - Stone - 15″ high ▷

Portrait of Anna - 1942 - Terracotta - 11″ high

16

Composition - 1943 - Plaster - 6″ x 8″ - Color by Fernand Léger

18

Constellation - 1943 - Plaster - 6″ x 8″ - Color by Fernand Léger

Dancers - 1943 - Plaster - 6″ x 8″ - Color by Fernand Léger

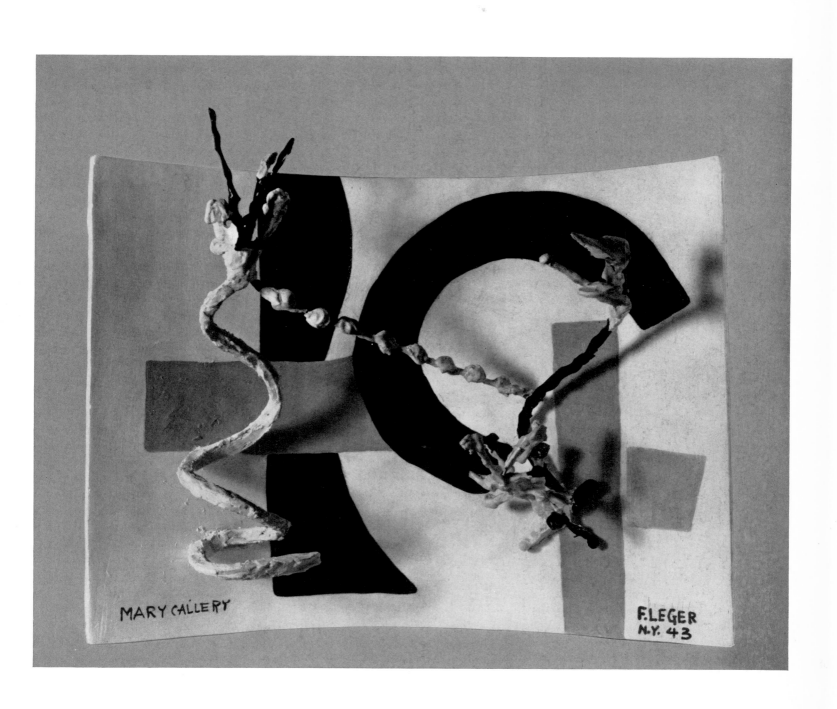

Composition - 1943 - Plaster - 6″ x 8″ - Color by Fernand Léger

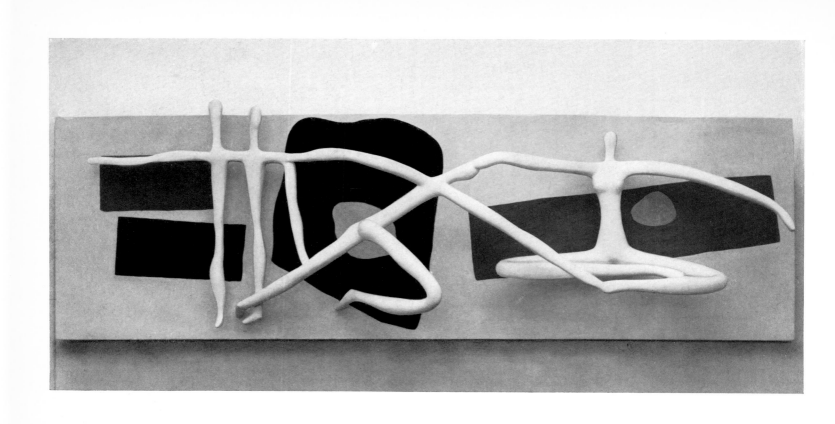

Mural Composition - 1949 - Plaster - 18″ x 57″ - Panel design by Fernand Léger

Standing Woman - 1949 - Plaster
43 $^1/_2$″ x 18″ - Panel design by
Fernand Léger

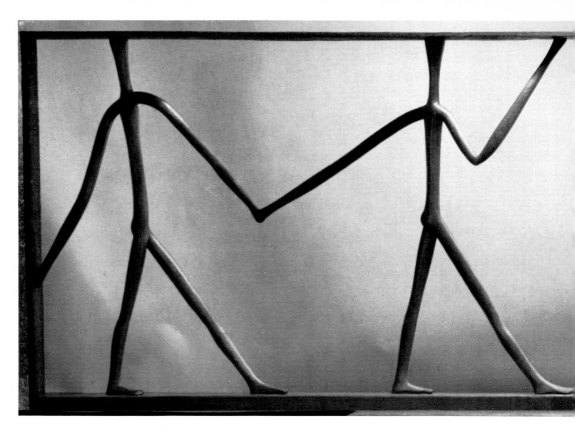

Amity - 1947 - Bronze - 5′ x 16′

Study for Amity - 1946 - Bronze - 7³/₄″ x 26″

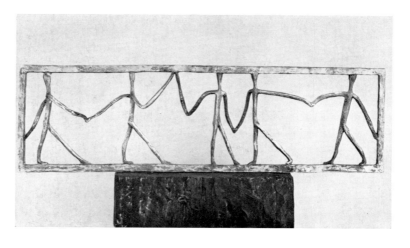

Amity

◁ Portrait of Severin - 1949 - Plaster - 18″ high

The Poet - 1945 - Bronze - 15″ high

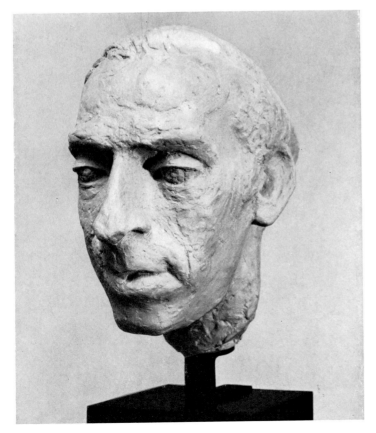

Portrait of a Flamenco Dancer - 1945 - Terracotta - 12″ high

Portrait of Georgia O'Keeffe - 1946 - Bronze - 12″ high

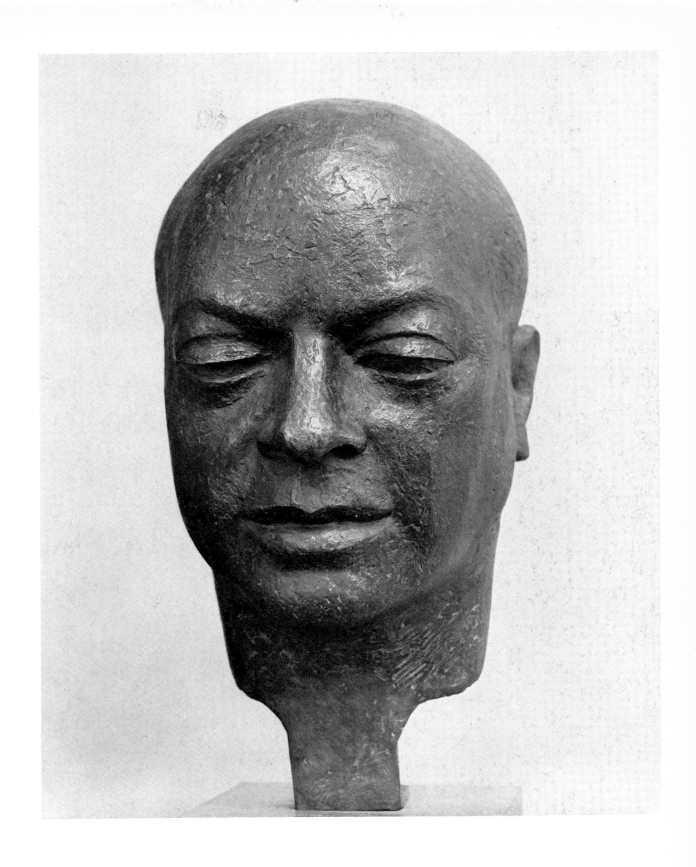

Portrait of Curt Valentin · 1946 · Bronze · 12″ high

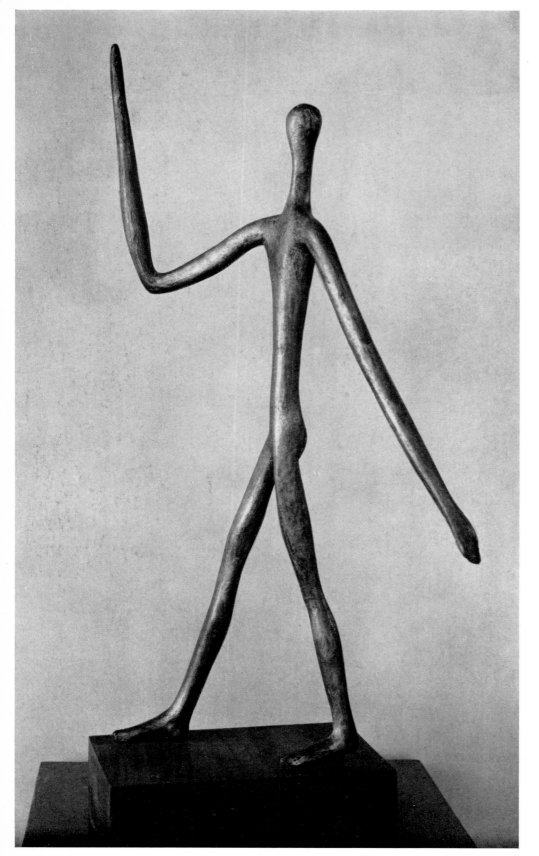

Study for St. Francis - 1947
Bronze - 20″ high

The Curve - 1947 - Bronze - 23″ high

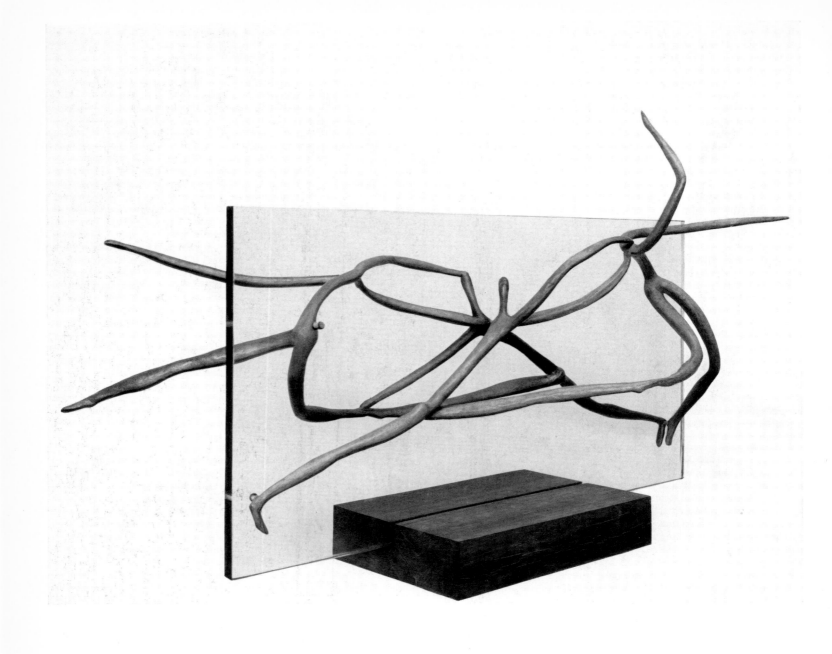

Composition on Glass - 1947 - Bronze - 24″ x 48″

Fish in Reeds - 1948 - Bronze - $12\,^{3}/_{4}'' \times 15\,^{1}/_{2}''$

Fish in Reeds - Painted

Two Sailors - 1948 - Bronze - 27″ high ▷

Ariel - 1948 - Bronze - 24 1/2″ high

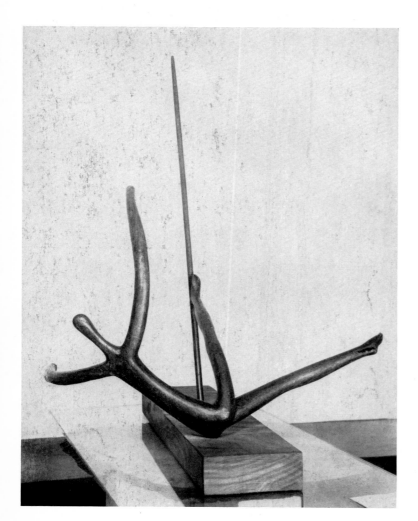

Woman in Space - 1948 - Bronze and glass - 32 ¹/₂″ × 96″

School of Fish - 1948 - Bronze - 8¹/₂″ x 15″

Portrait of Pamela - 1945 - Bronze - 15″ high

Portrait of Peter Ascoli - 1949 - Bronze - 15″ high

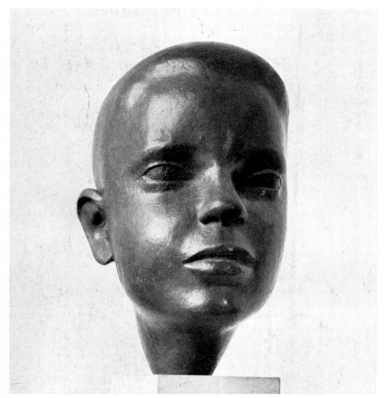

Portrait of Puma - 1948 - Bronze - 13 ¹/₃″ high ▷

38

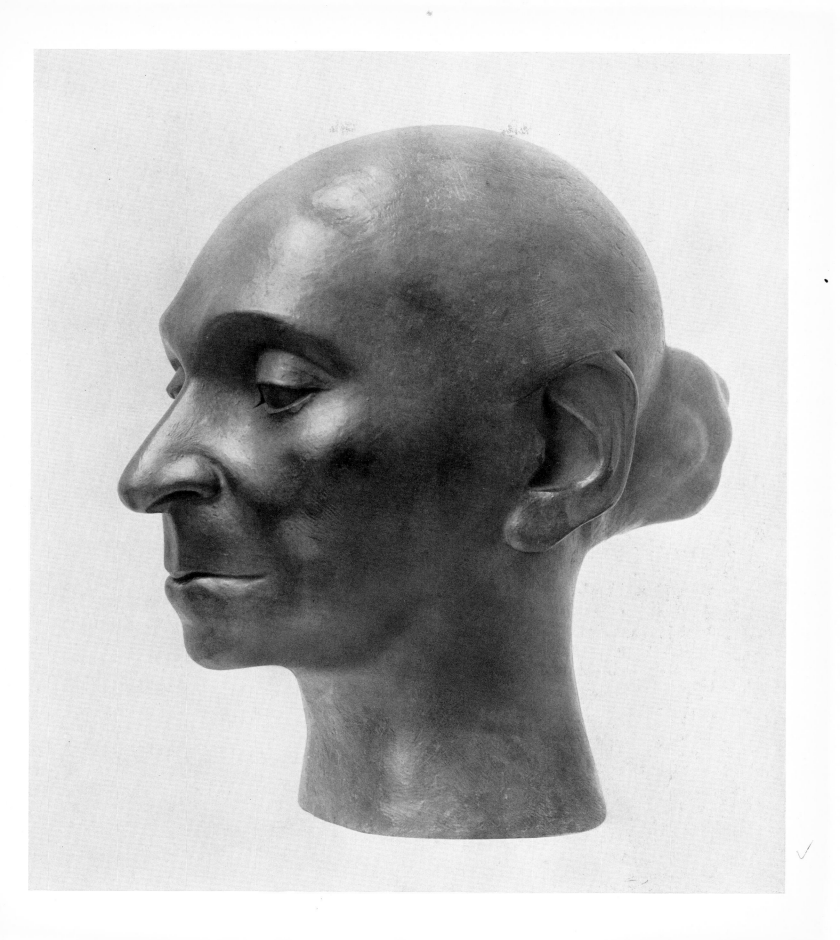

Study for Pyramid - 1949 - Bronze - 27 $1/2''$ high

Pyramid - 1949 - Bronze - 53″ high ▷

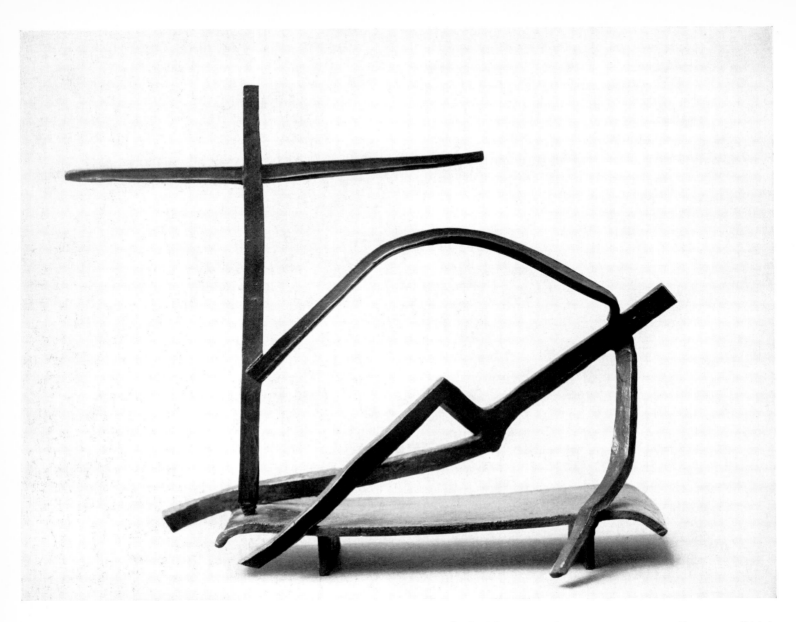

Study for Tomorrow is a Mystery - 1949 - Bronze - 7″ high

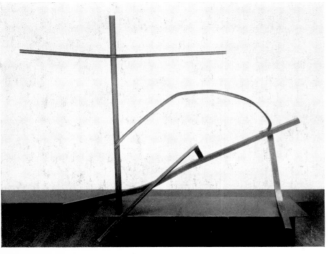

Tomorrow is a Mystery - 1949 - Iron - 70″ high

42

Study for Equilibrist - 1949
Bronze - 23 ½″ high

Douglas - 1949 - Bronze - 13 ½″ × 19″

Equilibrist - 1949 - Iron
72″ high

Mural Composition - 1949 - Bronze - 18″ x 57″

47   Conversation - 1949 - Bronze - 7″ high

Exposition Sculpture - 1949 - Iron - 42 ½″ high

Standing Woman - 1949
Plaster - 43 1/2″ x 18″

Daedalus - 1949 - Plaster - 25 ¹/₂″ high

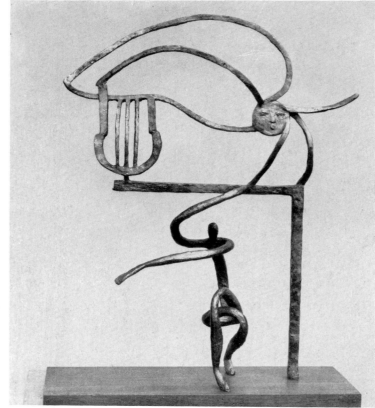

Above left:
St. Francis with Birds - 1951 - Bronze - 12″ high

Above right:
Eurydice - 1951 - Bronze - 20 ¼″ high

Below:
Study for Orpheus - 1951 - Bronze - 12 ¾″ high

Page 53:
Orpheus - 1951 - Bronze - 39 ½″ high

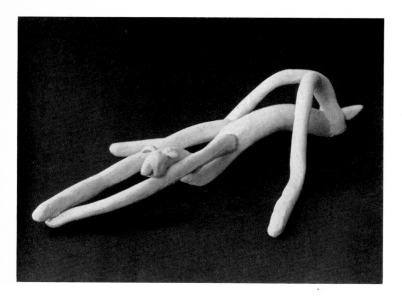

Piet - 1951 - Terracotta - 12 ¹/₂" long

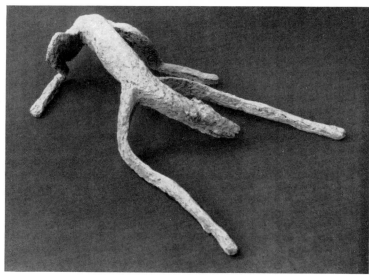

Piet - 1951 - Bronze - 14" long

Sleeping Dog - 1951 - Marble - 8" x 13¹/₂"

Puppies - 1951 - Terracotta - 6" long

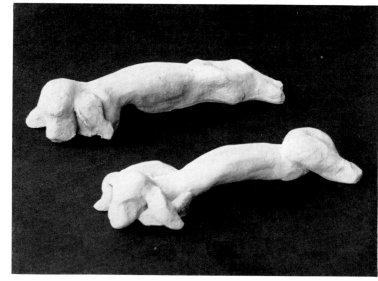

A Summer's Afternoon II - 1953 - Bronze - 7¹/₂″ long

A Summer's Afternoon I - 1951 - Bronze - 5 ¹/₂″ high

The Young Diana I - 1953 - Bronze - 16 ¹/₂″ long

Study for Young Diana II - 1954 - Bronze - 5 ¹/₈″ x 8″

The Young Diana II - 1952 - Bronze - 60" x 96"

Dog from Young Diana II - 1952 - Bronze - 30" high

Birds from Acrobats with Birds - 1952 - Bronze - 8″ x 15″

Acrobats with Birds - 1952 - Bronze - 52″ high ▷

Study for Acrobats with Birds - 1952 - Bronze - 17″ high

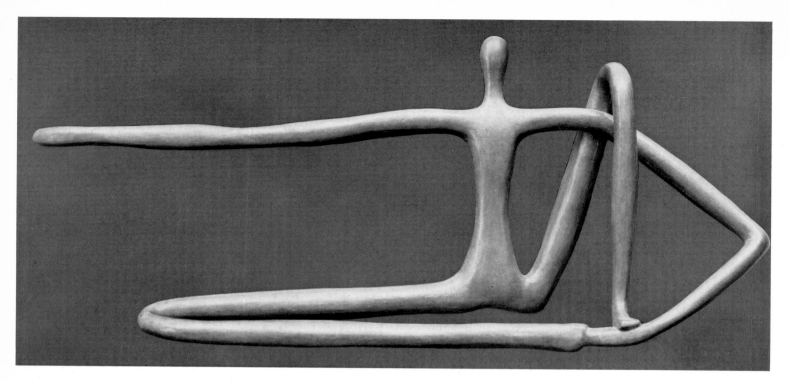

Espaliered Figure - 1952 - Bronze - 18″ x 40″

Seated Figure - 1947/52 - Bronze - 41″ high ▷

Two Figures - 1949 - Bronze - 12″ x 7″

Portrait of
Mrs. Marcus Bassevitch
1954 - Stone - 15″ high

Portrait of
Wallace K. Harrison
1954 · Bronze · 14″ high

Portrait of Richard B. Mellon · 1955 · Basalt · 18″ high

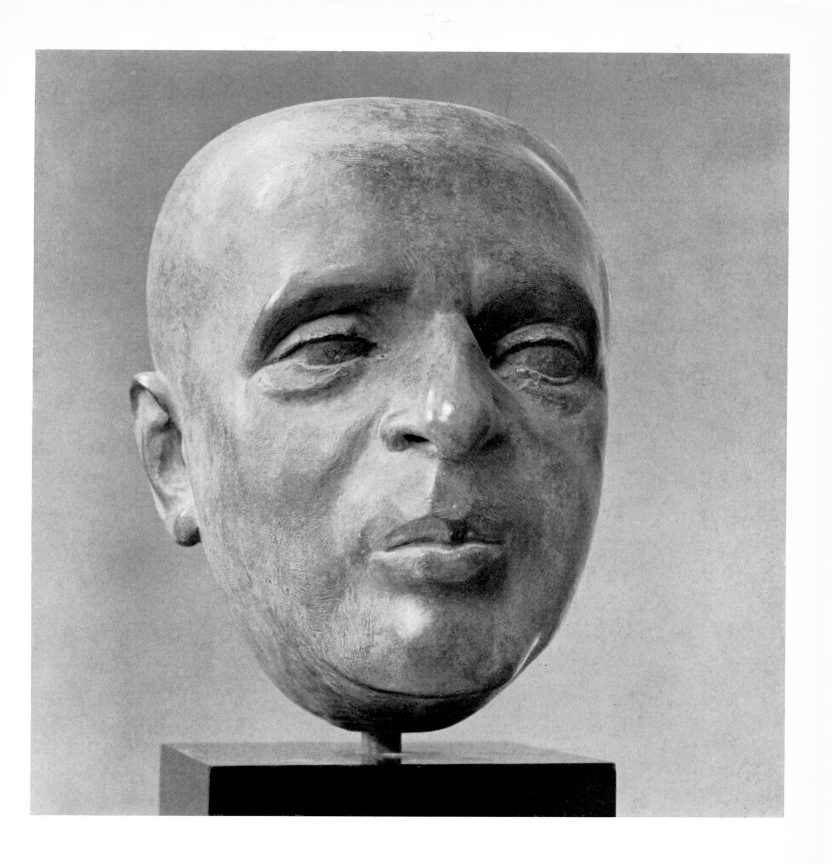

Portrait of J. B. Neumann - 1950 - Bronze - 10¹/₂″ high

Three Birds in Flight (model) - 1953 - Bronze - 2′ x 2′   66

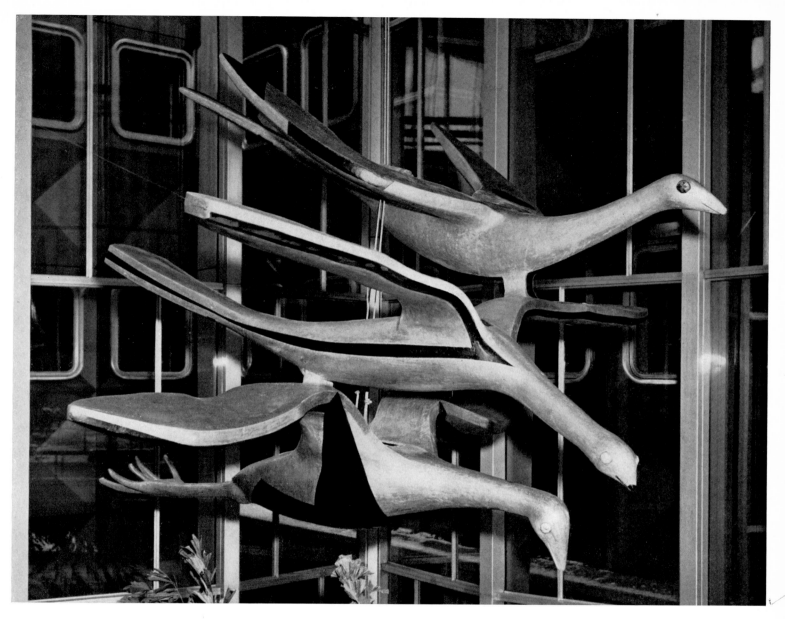

Three Birds in Flight - 1953 - Painted aluminum - 12' x 12'

Study for Three Birds in Flight - 1953 - Bronze - 6" long

Sons of Morning - 1953 - Bronze - 8′ long

Tancredi and Clorinda I - 1953 - Bronze - 16″ high

Tancredi and Clorinda II - 1953 - Bronze - 16" high

Constellation I - 1953 - Bronze - 5″ high

Constellation II (model) - 1953 - Bronze - 5 ³/₄″ high

Constellation II - 1955 - Painted aluminum - 40″ × 44″

Constellation II

Acrobats. Study for a Monument - 1954
Bronze - 3′ 6″ high

Acrobats. Monument - 1955 - Steel - 8′ high ▷

Acrobats. Study for a Monument (model) - 1953 - Bronze - 10″ high   72

Three studies for Ballet - 1953/54 - Bronze - 18″ long

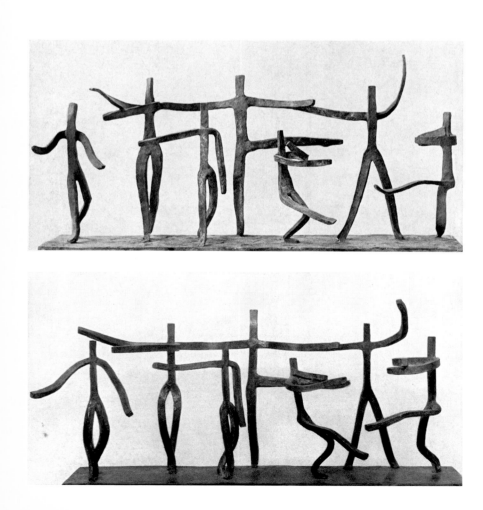

Page 76: Ballet - 1954 - Bronze - 42″ long

Study for Libellule - 1954 - Bronze - 3 ¹/₂″ high

Raphael - 1954 - Bronze - 2′ 4″ high

Study for Raphael - 1954 - Bronze - 6 ¾″ long   Fish in Reeds II - 1954 - Bronze - 12″ x 9 ½″ ▷

The Fables of La Fontaine (model) - 1954 - Bronze - 20″ long

The Fables of La Fontaine (detail)

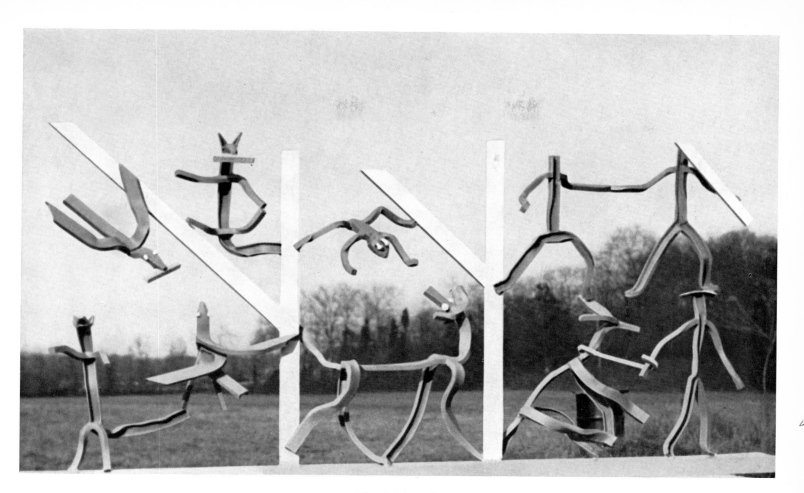

The Fables of La Fontaine (¹/₄ scale) – 1954 – Painted steel – 2′ 5″ x 5′

The Fables of La Fontaine (detail)

The Fables of La Fontaine - 1954 - Painted steel - 9′ 7″ x 20′

Portrait of Benjamin Fairless - 1954 - Basalt - 24″ high

Portrait of Colin Mackenzie · 1954 · Marble · 14″ high

The Seven - 1956 - Bronze - 34″ x 39″ ▷

The Seven (model) - 1955 - Bronze - 15″ high

Seascape. Study for a Gate - 1955 - Bronze
7³/₄″ x 17¹/₂″

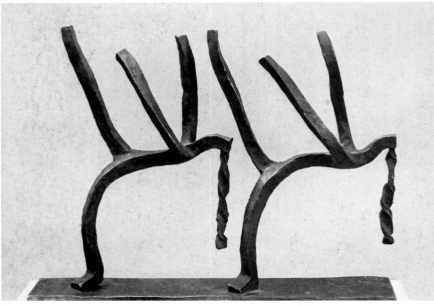

Sylvan Notions - 1956 - Bronze - 9¹/₂″ x 7″ ▷

Dancers - 1955 - Bronze - 12¹/₂″ x 2¹/₂″   90

Mother and Child (model) - 1956 - Bronze - 6″ x 7″

Mother and Child - 1957 - Bronze - 8′ long

94

Above:
Frog - 1956 - Bronze - 15″ x 13⅓″

Below left:
Frog - 1956 - Painted steel - 4′ long

Below right:
Frog - 1956 - Painted steel - 24″ x 18″

Page 94:
Bremen Town Musicians - 1956
Bronze - 15″ x 7½″

The Flirt (model) - 1957 - Bronze - 4″ × 4″

The Flirt - 1957 - Bronze - 22″ x 17″

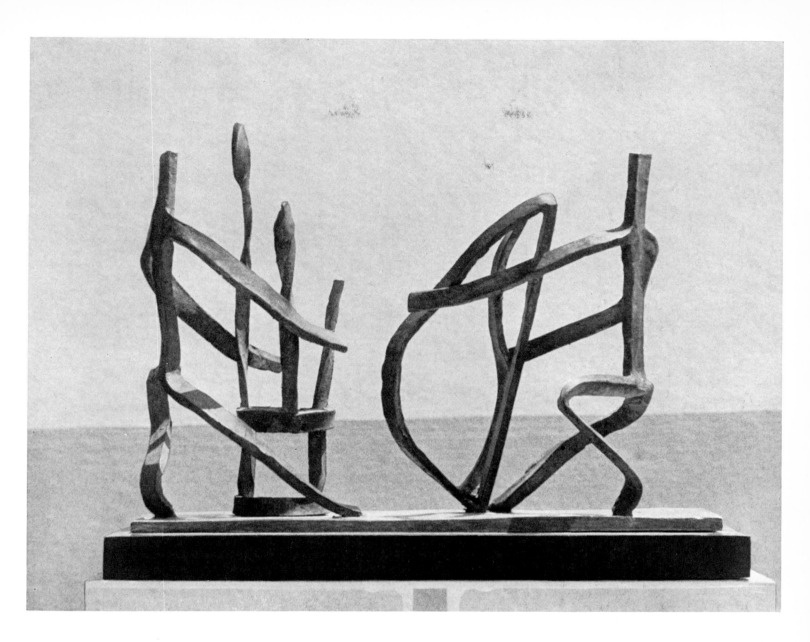

◁ Tara - 1957 - Bronze - 10 1/2" x 6 1/2"

Two Musicians - 1957 - Bronze - 10 1/4" x 4"

The Maze No. 1 - 1957 - Bronze - 10″ x 12″

The Maze No. 3 - 1957 - Brass - 10″ x 12″

The Maze No. 4 - 1957 - Bronze - 39″ high ▷

Joust - 1957 - Copper, steel and brass - 34″ x 17″ ▷

Pirouette - 1957 - Bronze - 13 1/2″ x 7 1/2″

Composition with Tendrils - 1957 - Painted steel ▷
and brass - 58″ x 40″

East Wind - 1957 - Bronze - 17″ x 12 1/2″

Composition with Tendrils (model) - 1957 - Bronze - 16 1/2″ x 12″

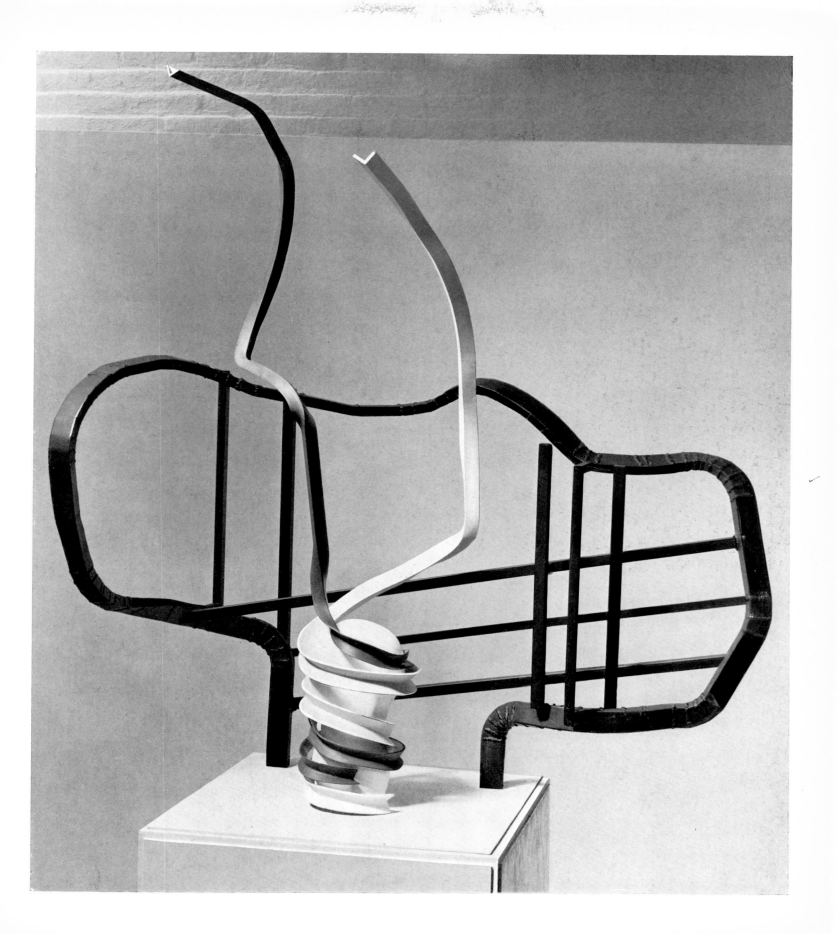

The Chase - 1957 - Bronze - Dog 4″, birds 1 ¹/₂″

The Finish Line - 1957 - Bronze - 10¹/₂″ x 4³/₄″

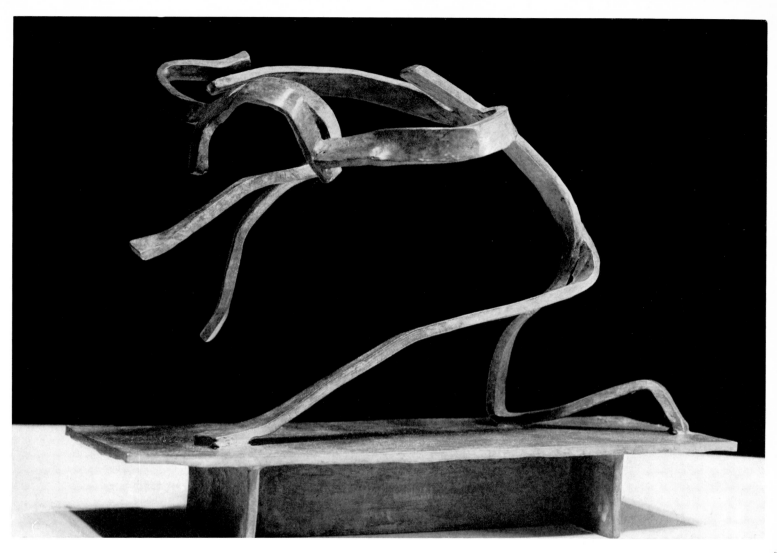

Somersault - 1958 - Bronze - 8″ x 10″

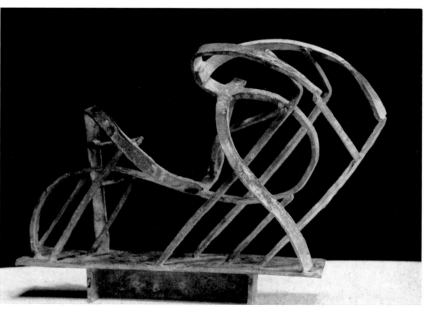

Personage in Rain - 1958 - Bronze - 9″ x 10 1/2″

Fountain - 1958 - Bronze - 9 1/2′ high ▷

Abstract Composition - 1957 - Bronze - 7 1/2″ x 7″

Composition - 1959 - Bronze - 9″ x 8 ¹/₂″ x 8″

Study for a Park Bench - 1959 - Bronze - 3 ¾″ x 6 ½″ x 2″

Mary Callery sait pertinemment que pour créer dans l'art l'état intersubjectif, émotion de l'artiste - réaction du spectateur, il est indispensable de réserver au réel tous ses droits. Cela malgré ses sympathies pour l'art non figuratif, auquel vont d'ailleurs souvent ses préférences quand il s'agit de l'oeuvre d'autrui. Seulement sitôt qu'elle s'engage dans une sculpture elle se rend solidaire de l'art qui guette la réalité et observe ses variations avec une curiosité inlassable. C'est qu'elle est sans aucun doute persuadée que si forte que soit son aspiration à laisser toute liberté à ses représentations, à les décharger de toute responsabilité à l'égard des modèles et à leur imposer par là une expression spécifique, son oeuvre, comme toute oeuvre d'art, pour avoir quelque chance de survivre, ne saurait être autre qu'une oeuvre à l'origine de laquelle président le réel et le mystère, non préparés par avance ni préalablement combinés, ni distincts l'un de l'autre.

Son expérience, fondée sur des preuves quotidiennes d'une évidence irrésistible, lui fait un devoir de réagir contre l'état presque chaotique de l'art actuel, au développement duquel rien n'est plus dangereux que l'activité brouillonne et inconsidérée d'un assez grand nombre d'artistes, préoccupés avant tout de donner l'illusion de l'originalité, sans réfléchir qu'il n'est d'illusion qui, tôt ou tard, ne se dissipe. Aussi dans chacune de ses oeuvres elle fait opérer son imagination conjointement avec ses modèles, dont elle tient à sauvegarder et les apparences simplifiées par la synthèse et les caractères les plus distinctifs.

On se tromperait toutefois du tout au tout en se figurant que ses sculptures ont subi une soumission totale au réel. L'art réaliste est déterminé par une adaptation entière aux seules valeurs de l'apparence du modèle, alors que l'artiste voit celui-ci simultanément sous son aspect physique et dans la perspective de ses propres catégories mentales et de toute sa gamme affective. Il en résulte que par rapport au modèle Callery prend chaque fois ses distances, souvent même elle s'attache à le mettre vivement en question.

On ne s'avancerait donc pas trop en assurant que dans ses oeuvres le monde extérieur et la réalité individuelle ne s'annulent jamais l'un l'autre mais se composent jusqu'à porter souvent l'oeuvre à une forte cohésion interne. La distance entre le modèle et l'image qu'elle en a tirée varie d'une sculpture à l'autre. Tantôt les choses sont appréhendées par elle de façon immédiate, tantôt suggérées dans leurs manifestations les plus lointaines.

Dès lors on conçoit que l'artiste ait modelé des figures où elle n'entend pas se couper de la réalité. Cela est valable pour toutes ses oeuvres tant pour les modèles vivants que les autres. Les sculptures exécutées par Callery en 1959 et 1960 nous apportent la preuve convaincante qu'elle peut avoir avec les signes une relation aussi complexe qu'avec le monde des personnes et des bêtes: femmes, acrobates, animaux tirés des fables de La Fontaine.

Dans ses dernières oeuvres le répertoire antérieur fait place aux caractères de l'écriture non pas en raison de la simplicité relative de leur tracé mais de la liberté qu'ils octroient au sculpteur de poursuivre un nombre infini de combinaisons de formes.

L'idée d'un recours aux signes n'a rien qui puisse surprendre. Les hommes ne cessent de communiquer au moyen de signes, car sont à n'en pas douter des signes aussi bien les lettres de l'écriture, que l'alphabet des sourds-muets, les rites symboliques, les mouvements des bras et des mains au cours des cérémonies religieuses, les emblèmes et les attributs, les gestes de politesse et j'en passe. L'art lui-même ne s'est-il pas toujours proposé la transcription plus ou moins conforme des signes au sein de la vie? C'est qu'en même temps que le signe est imprégné de sens, qu'il est le symbole du sentiment et de l'idée, il est aussi l'expression de la réalité. Il s'ensuit que les formes des signes concernent l'art au plus haut point. Celui qui possède la faculté de les regarder avec attention y découvre des virtualités esthétiques nombreuses. Les squelettes séméiologiques de l'écriture traités par Callery selon les données artistiques subissent des permutations, des implications réciproques, des exclusions et des distorsions de leurs formes telles que finalement ils retrouvent la vie. Soumises au pouvoir exhaustif de l'art les données brutes des signes ressortent sous de nouveaux jours, par cela même qu'entre-temps ils sont devenus les équivalents des divers choix que les objets et les figures proposent à l'imagination de l'artiste et auxquels elle marque sans distinction de valeur un intérêt privilégié. Pour Callery le signe a le même pouvoir que les modèles vivants de produire des tensions dans les profondeurs de l'inconscient, de provoquer des stimulations inespérées, de contenir une foule de combinaisons d'ordre plastique. Ainsi se trouve posée d'une manière nette la question de l'équivalence entre le signe et la matière qui l'étoffe, de la possibilité pour tous les deux d'aller parfaitement de pair, de la disposition des caractères de l'écriture à produire des développements esthétiques insoupçonnés et à donner l'existence à des combinaisons sculpturales harmonieusement structurées. En mettant ainsi l'accent plastique sur l'insolite de leurs tracés venus du fond des millénaires, Callery a créé des oeuvres d'une remarquable richesse de formes, qui, tout au long de la transformation des caractères en

trouvailles artistiques, contraint avec une si grande autorité leurs diverses parties à s'in-
tégrer les unes dans les autres, qu'aussitôt les signes s'éteignent dans l'oeuvre pour réappa-
raître sous formes d'art.

L'on doit enfin signaler qu'avec ses dernières sculptures Callery démontre que la technique
des moyens d'expression ne saurait être acceptable que dans la mesure où elle est à même
d'exprimer le plus aigu et le meilleur de l'esprit de l'artiste ainsi que de ses états affectifs.
Cette triple déférence de Callery pour le réel, le signe et la technique jointe à l'élément
dynamique de son imagination, constituent les traits les plus importants de ses options
esthétiques. C'est par là que l'on peut le mieux prendre la mesure de son oeuvre, projeter
un vif éclairage sur ses formes à la fois traditionnelles et très élargies, surprendre la vie
cachée mais active de l'artiste qui s'y trouve impliquée.

Christian Zervos

Mary Callery knows from experience that to create the "intersubjective" state in art (artist's emotion - spectator's reaction) one must grant reality all its due privileges. And this despite her sympathy for non-figurative art, which she often prefers when it is a question of other people's work. But as soon as she, herself, begins a sculpture she joins forces with the artists who lie in wait for reality, who observe its variations with untiring curiosity. This because she is doubtless persuaded that however strong may be her wish to bestow complete freedom on her works, to release them from all responsibility toward the model and in doing so to expose a specific expressiveness on them, her work, like all art that is to survive, must be presided over at birth by reality and mystery - but not concocted in advance, nor distinct one from the other.

Her experience, founded on the overwhelming evidence of everyday life, forces her to react against the almost chaotic state of today's art, whose development is seriously endangered by the thoughtless activity of many artists who wish above all to give the illusion of originality - forgetting that there is no illusion that does not fade away sooner or later. Thus in each of her works she brings her imagination and her model into play conjointly, insisting on preserving the model's appearance, simplified by synthesis, and its distinctive character.

It would be wrong, however, to imagine that her sculpture is completely submissive to reality. Realistic art is characterized by a total adjustment to the values of the model's appearance only, while the artist sees the model simultaneously in its physical aspect and in the perspective of his own mental categories and with the whole range of his emotions. So Callery, in each of her sculptures, keeps the model at arm's length, and often sharply calls its very existence into question.

Thus one may affirm that in her work the external world and the reality of the individual never cancel each other out, but on the contrary band together to give the work a strong internal cohesion. The distance between the model and the image she extracts from it varies from one sculpture to the next. Sometimes she seizes directly on appearances; sometimes she merely suggests their remotest aspects.

Hence we can see that the artist has no intention of isolating herself from reality in her work. This holds true for all her works - for those done from living models and for the others. The sculptures Callery did in 1959-60 are convincing proof that she can have with signs a relationship as complex as with the world of people and animals: women, acrobats, animals from La Fontaine's fables, for instance.

In this latest work she augments her repertory with figures that seem calligraphic not because of their relative simplicity of outline, but because of the liberty they grant to the sculptor to pursue an infinite number of combinations.

There is nothing surprising in this recourse to signs. Men never stop communicating with signs, for not only are letters of the alphabet signs, but so are the sign language of the deaf, symbolic rituals, motions of hands and arms during religious ceremonies, emblems and badges, gestures of politeness and so on. And hasn't art itself always been involved with the more or less exact transcription of the signs that are at the very core of life? Just as the sign is impregnated with meaning, just as it is the symbol of feeling and idea, so is it also the expression of reality. Hence the forms of the signs are of the utmost concern to art. The person who possesses the gift of looking attentively at them can discover numerous aesthetic virtualities. The semeiological skeletons of the handwriting Callery uses as a subject undergo, according to the artistic *données*, permutations, reciprocal contradictions, exclusions and distortions of their forms so that they ultimately rediscover life. The signs, a raw material submitted to the force of Callery's art, emerge in a new light, just because they have become in the meantime the equivalents of the various choices that objects and figures have suggested to the artist's imagination, and on which she has brought to play a privileged attention which purposely ignores questions of "value".

For Callery the sign has the same power as a living model of creating tension in the depths of the unconscious, of provoking unexpected stimulations, of containing a host of formal combinations. Thus Callery neatly formulates the question of the equivalence of the sign and the matter that gives it substance, of the possibility for both of proceeding on an equal footing, of the arranging of calligraphic figures to produce unsuspected aesthetic progressions and to generate harmoniously structured sculptural combinations. By thus placing the accent on the strangeness of these outlines from the prehistoric past, Callery creates works of a remarkable formal richness, which, throughout the process of the transforming of letters into artistic *trouvailles,* forces their various elements to combine together, with an authority so great that the signs immediately disappear into the work to reappear as artistic forms.

Finally, it must be pointed out that in her latest sculptures Callery shows that the technique of the artistic medium is valuable only in so far as it is able to express the finest and intensest moments of the artist's mind and sensibility.

Callery's triple deference to reality, sign and technique, and the dynamic element of her imagination, constitute the most important qualities of her art. It is through them that one can best measure the scope of her work, illuminate its forms which are both traditional and highly evolved, and discover the hidden yet active life of the artist which informs her work.

Christian Zervos

Composition 1 - 1960 - Steel and brass - 8 ³/4″ x 8 ³/4″ x 6″

◁ Composition 3 - 1960 - Steel
and brass - 10 ³/₄″ x 7″ x 11 ¹/₄″

Composition 4 - 1960 - Steel
and brass - 7 ³/₄″ x 10″ x 9 ¹/₄″

Composition 5 - 1960 - Steel
and brass - 7 ³/₄″ x 12 ¹/₂″ x 10″

Composition 6 - 1960 - Steel and brass - 10 ″ x 8 ″ x 12 ¹/₂ ″

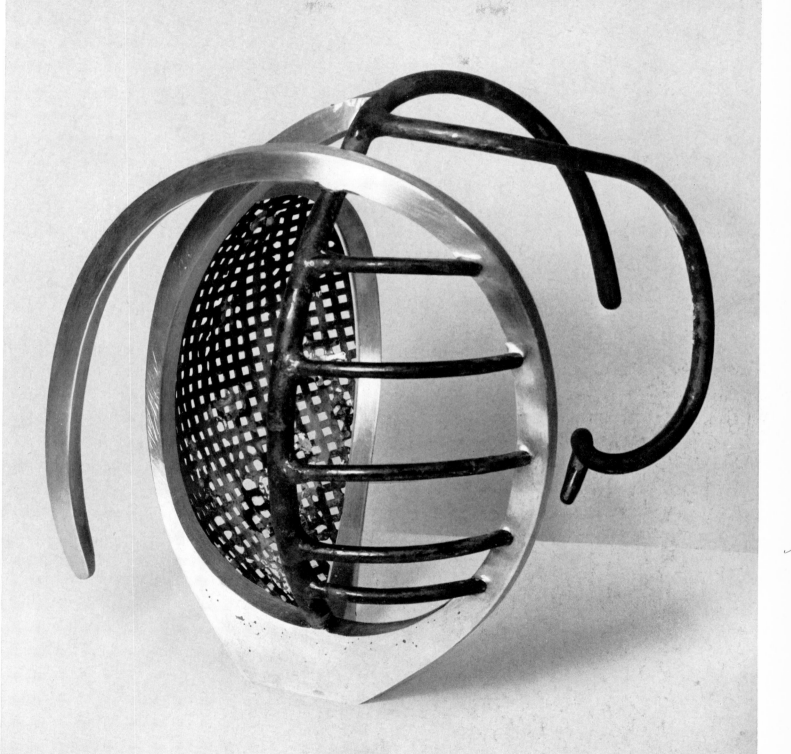

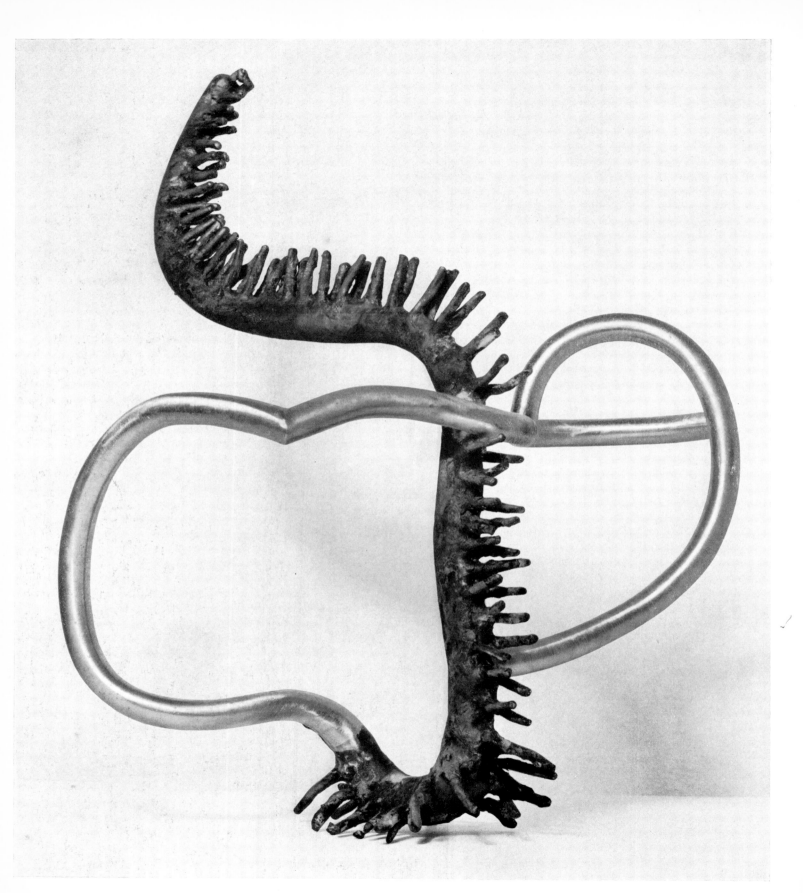

◁ Composition 8 - 1960 - Steel
and brass - 14″ x 9″ x 9″

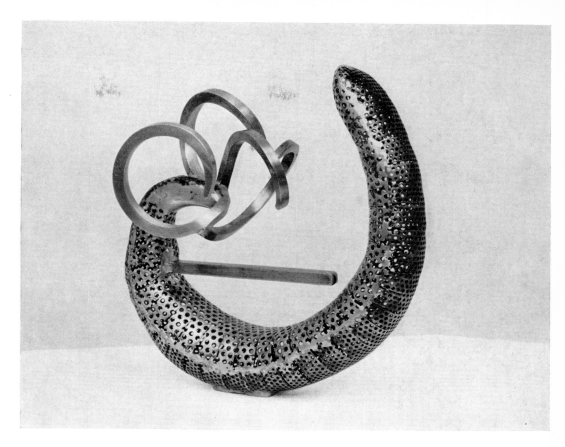

Composition 9 - 1960 - Steel
and brass - 9″ x 8 1/4″ x 2 3/4″

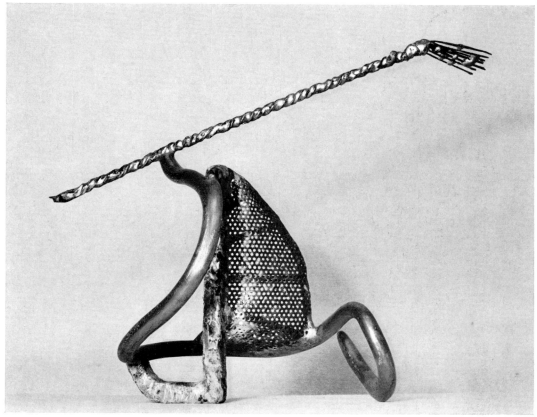

Composition 10 - 1960 - Steel
and brass - 10″ x 13″ x 6 3/4″

Composition 11 - 1960 - Steel and brass - 6 ³/₄ ″ x 10 ″ x 9 ″

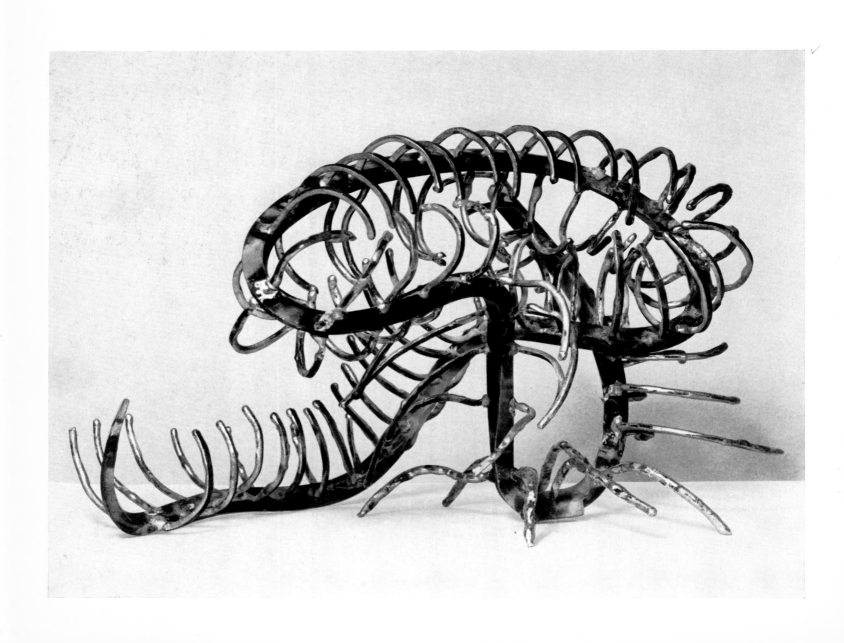

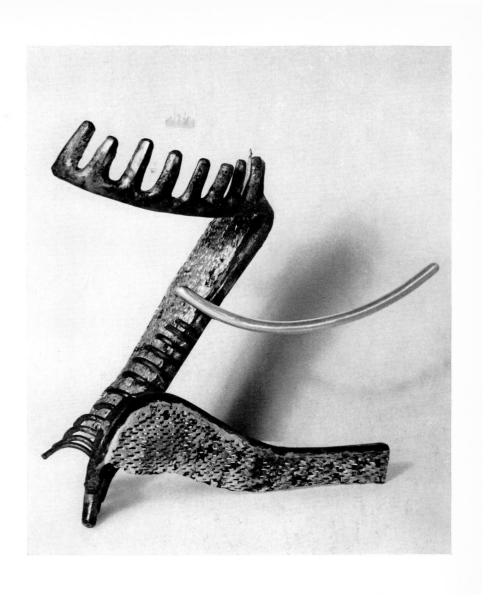

Composition 12 - 1960 - Steel and brass - 11″ x 14″ x 5″

Composition 13 - 1960 - Brass - 10″ x 16″ x 8¾″

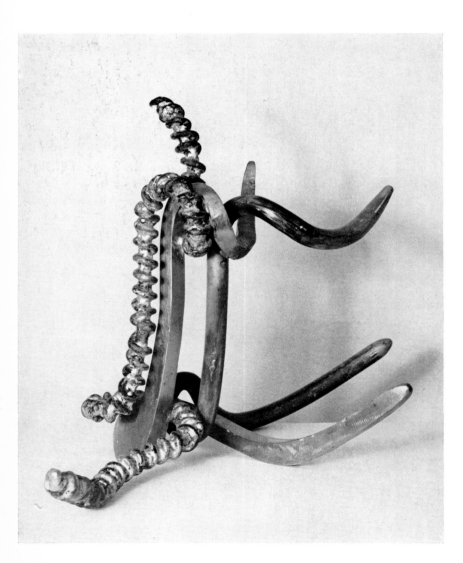

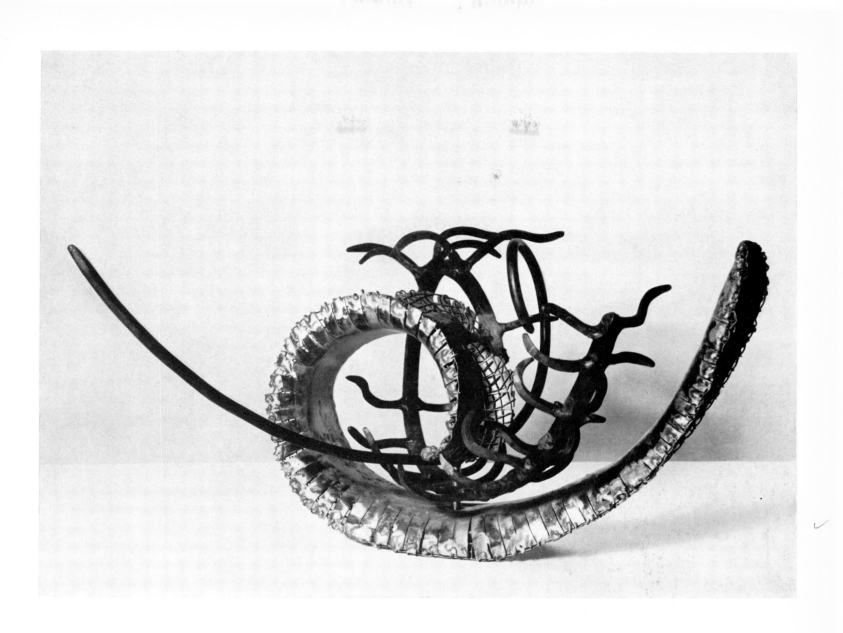

Composition 14 - 1960 - Steel and brass - 6 ¹/₂″ x 10 ¹/₄″ x 12″

Composition 15 - 1960 - Brass
8″ x 9¼″ x 5¼″

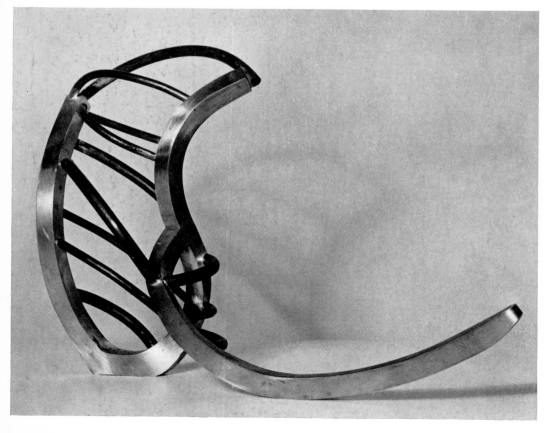

Composition 16 - 1960 - Steel
and brass - 7¾″ x 11½″ x 4″

Composition 17 - 1960 - Brass ▷
9¼″ x 10″ x 9″

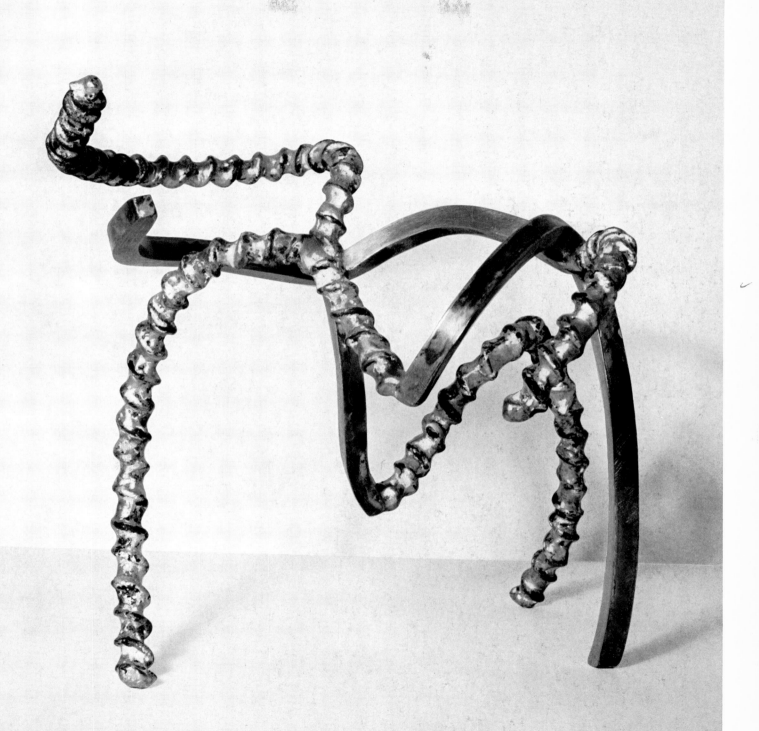

Composition 18 - 1960 - Steel and brass - 11 ¾″ x 11″ x 5″

Composition 19 - 1960 - Steel and brass - 7″ x 15″ x 9″

Composition 20 - 1960 - Steel - 10 ¹/₄″ x 16″ x 11″

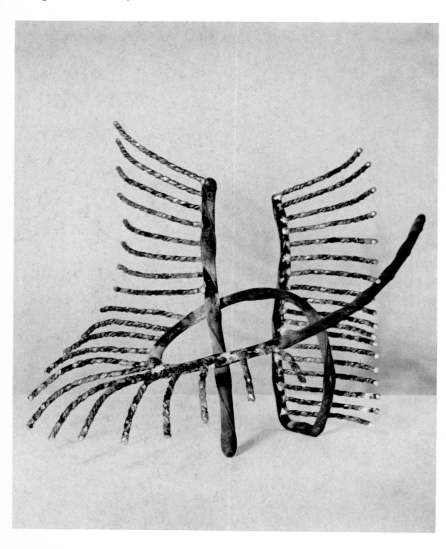

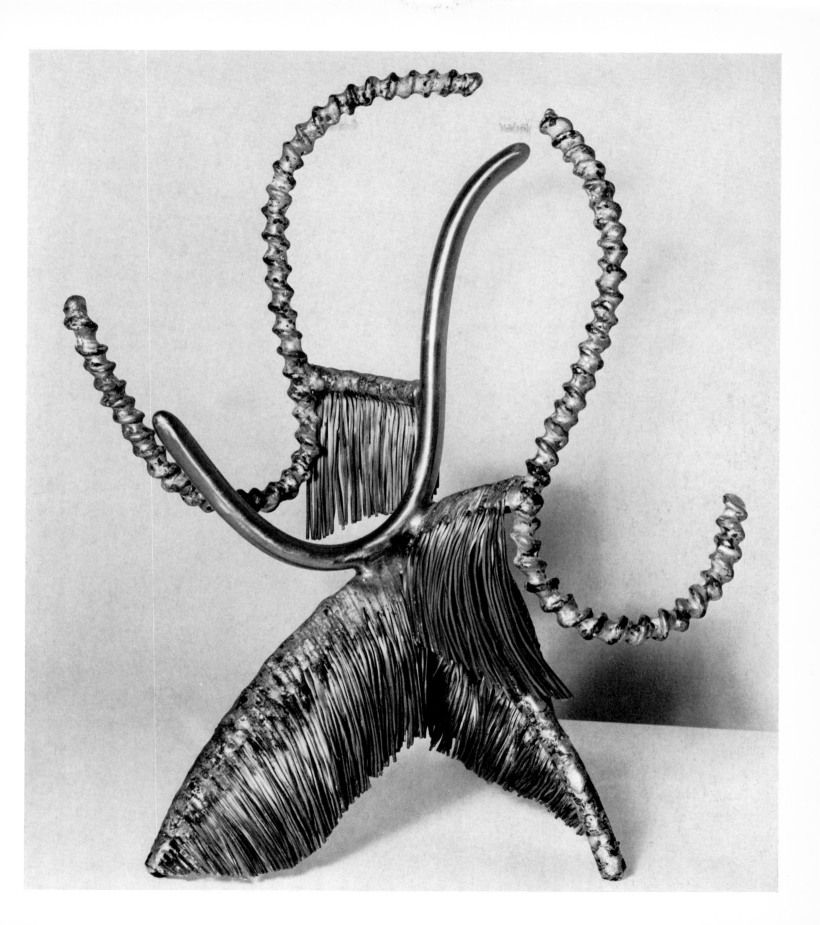

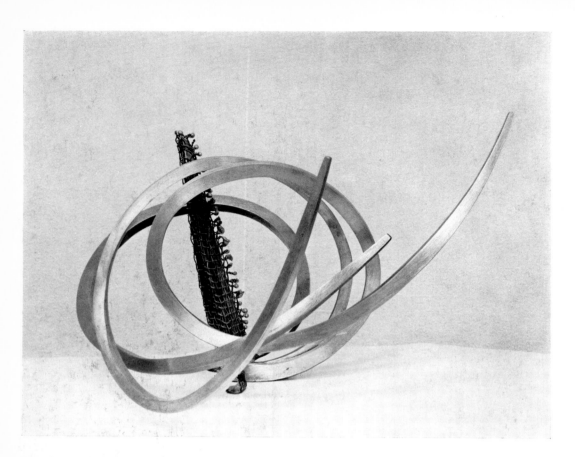

Composition 24 - 1960 - Steel
and brass - 7″ x 12 ½″ x 10 ½″

Composition 25 - 1960 - Steel
and brass - 7″ x 15″ x 5″

Composition 26 - 1960 - Steel ▷
and brass - 7 ½″ x 6 ½″ x 6″

Composition 27 - 1960 - Steel and brass - 10 " x 9 $^{1}/_{2}$ " x 10 $^{1}/_{2}$ "

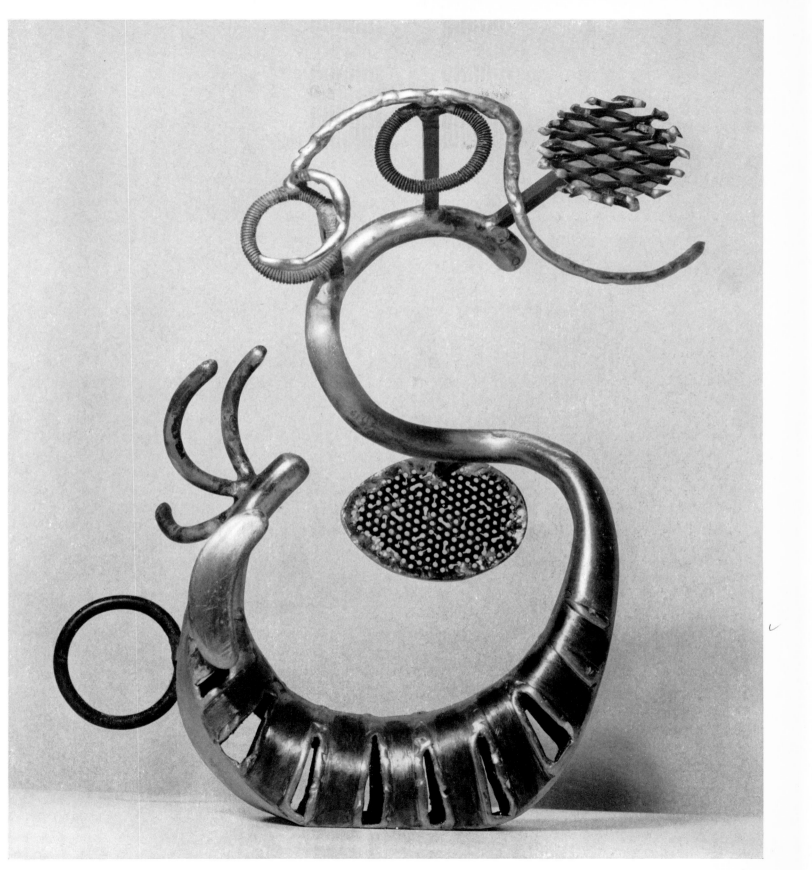

1942

1 Musician. 1942.
12 3/4″ high. Bronze, 1/1 owned by artist.
Reproduced p. 1.

2 Circus Riders. 1942.
24 1/2″ high. Bronze, 1/1 collection
Dr. David Levy, New York.
Reproduced p. 2.

3 Plant. 1942.
9 1/4″ long. Bronze, 1/1 owned by artist.
Reproduced p. 2.

4 Horse. 1942.
47 1/2″ high. Bronze, 1/2 The Museum of
Modern Art, New York; 2/2 collection
Mr. Eben Draper, Wakefield, R. I.
Reproduced p. 3.

5 Reclining Figure (model). 1942.
10″ long. Bronze, 1/3 collection Mr. and
Mrs. Robert Leonhardt, Huntington, N.Y.;
2/3 collection Mrs. Etta Steinberg,
New York; 3/3 collection
Mrs. George Siemonn, New York.

6 Reclining Figure (1/4 scale). 1942.
2 1/2′ long. Bronze, 1/1 owned by artist.
Reproduced p. 4.

7 Portrait of Harry Mathews. 1942.
12″ high. Bronze, 1/1 owned by artist.
Reproduced p. 14.

8 Head of a Girl. 1942.
11″ high. Terracotta, 1/1 collection
Miss Philomena Guilbaud, London.
Bronze, 1/1 owned by artist.
Reproduced p. 15.

9 Portrait of Anna. 1942.
11″ high. Terracotta, 1/1 owned by artist.
Reproduced p. 16.

1943

10 The Tree. 1943.
41″ high. Bronze, 1/1 collection
Mr. Sturges Ingersoll, Philadelphia.
Reproduced p. 6.

11 Branches. 1943.
23 1/2″ x 36″. Bronze, 1/1 owned by artist.
Reproduced p. 7.

12 Butterfly. 1943.
6″ high. Bronze, 1/3 collection Miss Josephine Plows-Day, Boston, Mass.;
2/3 collection Mr. Peter Ascoli, New York;
3/3 owned by artist.

13 Moncha. 1943.
12″ high. Terracotta, 1/1 owned by artist.

14 Portrait of B. D. 1943.
14 1/2″ high. Bronze, 1/1 owned by artist.

15 Composition. Color by Fernand Léger. 1943.
6″ x 8″. Plaster, 1/1 Musée Léger, Biot, A.M.
Reproduced p. 18.

16 Constellation. Color by Fernand Léger. 1943.
6″ x 8″. Plaster, 1/1 Musée Léger, Biot, A.M.
Reproduced p. 19.

17 Dancers. Color by Fernand Léger. 1943.
6″ x 8″. Plaster, 1/1 Musée Léger, Biot, A.M.
Reproduced p. 20.

18 Composition. Color by Fernand Léger. 1943.
6″ x 8″. Plaster, 1/1 Musée Léger, Biot, A.M.
Reproduced p. 21.

1944

19 Reclining Figure. 1944.
105″ long. Bronze, 1/1 collection
Mr. and Mrs. Robert Leonhardt,
Huntington, N.Y. Reproduced p. 5.

20 Dancers. 1944.
48″ high. Bronze, 1/1 owned by artist.
Reproduced p. 7.

21 Constellation. 1944.
48″ high. Plaster, destroyed.
Reproduced p. 8.

22 Small Ballet. 1944.
12″ x 6 1/2″. Bronze, 1/3 collection
Mrs. L. Esteves Fernandes, Lisbon;
2/3 collection Josef Albers, New Haven,
Conn.; 3/3 owned by artist. Slight
variation in the three casts.
Reproduced p. 10.

23 Acrobats (model). 1944.
16 1/2″ high. Bronze, 1/3 collection
Judge Loew, Floral Park, N.Y.;
2/3 collection Mr. Max Abramovitz,
New York; 3/3 collection
Mrs. Serge Sachnoff, Washington, D. C.
Slight variation in the three casts.

1945

24 Acrobats. 1945.
44″ x 20″ x 24″. Bronze, 1/3 New York
University Art Collection; 2 + 3/3 owned
by artist. Reproduced p. 9.

25 Song of the Desert. 1945.
25″ high. Bronze, 1 + 2/2 owned by artist.
Reproduced p. 10.

26 Five Acrobats. 1945.
19″ high. Bronze, 1/1 collection
Mr. and Mrs. Richard Rodgers, New York.
Reproduced p. 11.

27 Portrait of Sally. 1945.
15″ high. Terracotta, 1/1 owned by artist.
Stone, 1/1 collection Mrs. Sally Pomeranz,
Lexington, Mass. Reproduced p. 17.

28 The Poet. 1945.
15″ high. Bronze, 1/2 collection
Madame Maria Martins, Rio de Janeiro;
2/2 collection Miss Josephine Plows-Day,
Boston, Mass. Reproduced p. 27.

29 Portrait of a Flamenco Dancer. 1945.
12″ high. Terracotta, 1/1 owned by artist.
Bronze, 1/1 collection Mr. Martinez,
New York. Reproduced p. 27.

30 Portrait of Pamela. 1945.
15″ high. Bronze, 1/3 collection
Mrs. Pamela Bradbourne, Tripoli, Lybia;
2/3 collection Mr. Oscar Nitzchke,
New York; 3/3 owned by artist.
Reproduced p. 38.

31 Seated Figure. 1945.
12 1/2″ high. Bronze, destroyed.

32 Study for Seated Ballet. 1945.
19 3/4″ x 13 1/2″. Bronze 1/1 owned by
artist. Reproduced p. 12.

1946

33 Seated Ballet. 1946.
64″ x 46″. Bronze, 1/1 collection
Mr. Harold Johnson, Louisville, Kentucky.
Reproduced p. 13.

34 Portrait of Georgia O'Keeffe. 1946.
12″ high. Bronze, 1/1 owned by artist.
Reproduced p. 28.

35 Portrait of Curt Valentin. 1946.
12″ high. Bronze, 1/1 owned by artist.
Reproduced p. 29.

36 Study for Amity. 1946.
7 3/4″ x 26″. Bronze, 1/5 collection Mr. and
Mrs. Burton Tremaine, Meriden, Conn.;
2/5 collection Mr. and Mrs. John Rood,
Minneapolis; 3/5 collection Mr. John Spring,
New York; 4/5 Detroit Institute of Arts;
5/5 North Shore Art Society, Long Island.
Reproduced p. 24.

1947

37 Amity. 1947.
5′ x 16′. Bronze, 1/1 owned by artist.
Reproduced p. 25.

38 Study for St. Francis. 1947.
20″ high. Bronze, 1/4 collection
Mr. Carlo Frua de Angeli, Milan;
2/4 collection Miss Josephine Plows-Day,
Boston, Mass.; 3/4 collection Mr. David
Thompson, Pittsburgh; 4/4 owned by
artist. Reproduced p. 30.

39 St. Francis. 1947.
9′ high. Plaster for bronze,
1/1 owned by artist.

40 The Curve. 1947.
23″ high. Bronze, 1/3 collection
Mrs. Arthur Hooper, Baltimore;
2/3 Cincinnati Art Museum;
3/3 Toledo Museum of Art.
Reproduced p. 31.

41 Composition on Glass. 1947.
24″ x 48″. Bronze, 1/1 collection
Mr. and Mrs. Burton Tremaine, Meriden,
Conn. Reproduced p. 32.

42 Seated Figure. 1947/52.
41″ high. Bronze, 1/1 owned by artist.
Reproduced p. 61.

1948

43 Fish in Reeds. 1948.
12 3/4″ x 15 1/2″. Bronze, 1/1 owned by artist.
Reproduced p. 33.

44 Ariel. 1948.
24 1/2″ high. Bronze, 1 + 2/2 owned by
artist. Reproduced p. 34.

45 Two Sailors. 1948.
27″ high. Bronze, 1/2 collection
Mr. and Mrs. Fred Lazarus, Cincinnati, Ohio;
2/2 owned by artist. Reproduced p. 35.

46 Study for Woman in Space. 1948.
7″ x 25″. Bronze and glass, 1/6 collection
M. Christian Zervos, Paris; 2/6 collection
Mr. John S. Newberry, Jr., Detroit;
3/6 collection Mr. and Mrs. Roy
J. Friedman, Chicago;
4-6/6 owned by artist.

47 Woman in Space. 1948.
32 1/2″ x 96″. Bronze and glass,
1/1 collection Mr. Fritz Glarner,
Huntington, N.Y. Reproduced p. 36.

48 School of Fish. 1948.
8 1/2″ x 15″. Bronze, 1/1 Addison Gallery,
Andover, Mass. Reproduced p. 37.

49 Portrait of Puma. 1948.
13 1/3″ high. Terracotta, 1 + 2/2 owned
by artist. Bronze, 1 + 2/2 owned
by artist. Reproduced p. 39.

1949

50 Mural Composition. 1949.
18″ x 57″. Bronze, 1/8 collection
Mrs. Max Ascoli, New York; 2/8 collection
Mr. Nelson A. Rockefeller, New York;
3/8 owned by artist. Same sculpture with
panel by Fernand Léger see Catalog
No. 51. Reproduced p. 46.

51 Mural Composition. 1949.
Panel design by Fernand Léger.
18″ x 57″. Plaster, 1/2 Musée Léger,
Biot, A. M.; 2/2 owned by artist. Bronze,
1/8 collection Mr. Gerald Gidwitz, Chicago;
2/8 collection Dr. and Mrs. Robert Levine,
Brightwater, N.Y.; 3/8 owned by artist.
Same sculpture without panel by Fernand
Léger see Catalog No. 50.
Reproduced p. 22.

52 Standing Woman. 1949.
43 1/2″ x 18″. Plaster, 1/2 collection
Mr. and Mrs. Todd Webb, New York;
2/2 owned by artist. Same sculpture with
panel by Fernand Léger see Catalog
No. 53. Reproduced p. 49.

53 Standing Woman. 1949.
Panel design by Fernand Léger.
43 1/2″ x 18″. Plaster, 1/2 Musée Léger,
Biot, A. M.; 2/2 owned by artist. Bronze,
1/8 owned by artist. Same sculpture
without panel by Fernand Léger see
Catalog No. 52. Reproduced p. 23.

54 Portrait of Severin. 1949.
18″ high. Plaster for bronze, 1/1 owned by
artist. Reproduced p. 26.

55 Portrait of Peter Ascoli. 1949.
15″ high. Marble, 1/1 collection
Mr. Peter Ascoli, New York. Bronze,
1/1 owned by artist. Reproduced p. 38.

56 Kneeling Figure. 1949.
8 1/2″ high. Bronze, 1/1 private collection.

57 Study for Pyramid. 1949.
27 1/2″ high. Bronze, 1/2 San Francisco
Museum of Art; 2/2 private collection.
Reproduced p. 40.

58 Pyramid. 1949.
53″ high. Bronze, 1/2 collection
Mr. and Mrs. Joseph Pulitzer, St. Louis;
2/2 owned by artist. Reproduced p. 41.

59 Study for Tomorrow is a Mystery. 1949.
7″ high. Bronze, 1/2 collection
Mr. and Mrs. Jean de Menil, Houston,
Texas; 2/2 San Francisco Museum of Art.
Slight variation in the two casts.
Reproduced p. 42.

60 Tomorrow is a Mystery. 1949.
70″ high. Iron, 1/1 owned by artist.
Reproduced p. 42.

61 Study for Equilibrist. 1949.
23 1/2″ high. Bronze, 1/2 Galerie Mai, Paris;
2/2 owned by artist. Slight variation in
the two casts. Reproduced p. 43.

62 Equilibrist. 1949.
72″ high. Iron, 1/1 owned by artist.
Reproduced p. 45.

63 Douglas. 1949.
13 1/2″ x 19″. Bronze, 1/1 owned by artist.
Reproduced p. 44.

64 Conversation. 1949.
7″ high. Bronze, 1/8 collection
Mr. Philip Johnson, New Canaan, Conn.;
2/8 collection Mrs. Simon Boosey,
New York; 3/8 collection
Mrs. Emily Heron, Pittsburgh;
4/8 collection Mrs. Nora Martins, Rio de
Janeiro; 5/8 collection
Mr. Carlo Frua de Angeli, Milan;
6/8 collection Mr. and Mrs. Marcus
Bassevitch, West Hartford, Conn.;
7/8 collection Mrs. Sidney Solomon,
New York. Reproduced p. 47.

65 Exposition Sculpture. 1949.
42 1/2″ high. Iron, 1/1 collection
Mr. Fritz Glarner, Huntington, N.Y.
Plaster, 1/1 owned by artist.
Reproduced p. 48.

66 Abstract Composition. 1949.
21″ x 43″. Bronze, iron and slate,
1/1 owned by artist.

67 Saint Michael. 1949.
4 1/2″ high. Bronze, 1/1 collection
Mrs. I. M. Sachs, New York.

68 Daedalus. 1949.
25 1/2″ high. Plaster, destroyed. Bronze,
1 + 2/2 owned by artist.
Reproduced p. 50.

69 Two Figures. 1949.
12″ x 7″. Bronze, 1/1 collection
Mrs. Gerald Wexler, New York.
Reproduced p. 60.

1950

70 Four Figures. 1950.
15″ x 37 1/2″. Bronze, 1 + 2/2
owned by artist.

71 Perhaps. 1950.
28″ high. Bronze, 1/2 collection
Mr. Oliver James, Phoenix, Arizona;
2/2 collection Mr. and Mrs. Otto L. Spaeth,
New York. Reproduced p. 51.

72 Portrait of J. B. Neumann. 1950.
10 1/2″ high. Terracotta, 1/1 owned by
artist. Bronze, 1/1 owned by artist.
Reproduced p. 65.

1951

73 St. Francis with Birds. 1951.
12″ high. Bronze, 1/1 owned by artist.
Reproduced p. 52.

74 Eurydice. 1951.
20 1/4″ high. Bronze, 1/2 Wadsworth
Atheneum, Hartford, Conn.;
2/2 owned by artist. Reproduced p. 52.

75 Study for Orpheus. 1951.
12 3/4″ high. Bronze, 1/4 collection
Mrs. J. D. Rockefeller III, New York;
2/4 San Francisco Museum of Art;
3/4 private collection; 4/4 owned by artist.
Reproduced p. 52.

76 Orpheus. 1951.
39 1/2″ high. Bronze, 1/3 collection
Mr. Nelson A. Rockefeller, New York;
2/3 collection Mr. Sturges Ingersoll,
Philadelphia; 3/3 owned by artist.
Reproduced p. 53.

77 Yolanda. 1951.
7 1/2″ high. Terracotta, 1/1 owned by artist.

78 Piet. 1951.
12 1/2″ long. Terracotta,
1/1 owned by artist. Reproduced p. 54.

79 Piet. 1951.
14″ long. Bronze, 1–3/3 owned by artist.
Reproduced p. 54.

80 Sleeping Dog. 1951.
8″ x 13 1/2″. Marble, 1/1 owned by artist.
Reproduced p. 54.

81 Puppies. 1951.
6″ long. Terracotta, 1/1 collection
Mr. and Mrs. Todd Webb, New York.
Reproduced p. 54.

82 A Summer's Afternoon I. 1951.
5 1/2″ high. Bronze, 1/1 collection
Mrs. J. D. Rockefeller III, New York.
Reproduced p. 55.

1952

83 Study for Young Diana I. 1952.
5 1/4″ x 16″. Plaster, owned by artist.

84 Study for Young Diana II. 1952.
5 1/8″ x 8″. Plaster, owned by artist.

85 The Young Diana II. 1952.
60″ x 96″. Bronze, 1/1 collection
Mr. Ted Weiner, Fort Worth, Texas.
Reproduced p. 57.

86 Dog from Young Diana II. 1952.
30″ high. Bronze, 1/8 collection
Mr. and Mrs. Richard Deutsch,
Greenwich, Conn.; 2/8 owned by artist.
Reproduced p. 57.

87 Study for Acrobats with Birds. 1952.
17″ high. Bronze, 1/1 collection
Mr. Marcus Rice, Laden, Missouri.
Reproduced p. 58.

88 Acrobats with Birds. 1952.
52″ high. Bronze, 1/8 collection
Mr. and Mrs. Lawrence Rockefeller,
New York; 2/8 collection
Mrs. E. J. Hudson, Houston, Texas;
3/8 owned by artist.
Reproduced p. 59.

89 Birds from Acrobats with Birds. 1952.
8″ x 15″. Bronze, 1/1 owned by artist.
Reproduced p. 58.

90 Espaliered Figure. 1952.
18″ x 40″. Bronze, 1/8 collection
Mr. and Mrs. Hazel Arnett, New York;
2/8 collection Mr. and Mrs.
Robert Leonhardt, Huntington, N.Y.
Reproduced p. 60.

1953

91 A Summer's Afternoon II. 1953.
7 1/2″ long. Bronze, 1/1 collection Mr. and
Mrs. E. J. Mathews, New York.
Reproduced p. 55.

92 The Young Diana I. 1953.
16 1/2″ long. Bronze, 1/2 collection Mr. and
Mrs. Richard Davis, Minneapolis, Minn.;
2/2 collection Mrs. Harold Levin,
New York. Slight variation in the two
casts. Reproduced p. 56.

93 Study for Three Birds in Flight. 1953.
6″ long. Bronze, 1/1 collection
Mr. and Mrs. Henrique Mindlin,
Rio de Janeiro. Reproduced p. 67.

94 Three Birds in Flight (model). 1953.
2′ x 2′. Painted plaster,
1/3 collection Mr. and Mrs. Wallace
K. Harrison, New York;
2/3 collection Mr. Fritz Close, Pittsburgh;
3/3 owned by artist.
Bronze, 1/8 owned by artist.
Reproduced p. 66.

95 Three Birds in Flight. 1953.
12′ x 12′. Painted aluminum, 1/1 Aluminium
Company of America, Pittsburgh.
Reproduced p. 67.

96 Sons of Morning. 1953.
8′ long. Bronze, 1/2 collection Mrs. Jane
Owens, Harmony, Indiana; 2/2 owned
by artist. Reproduced p. 68.

97 Tancredi and Clorinda I. 1953.
16″ high. Bronze, 1/1 owned by artist.
Reproduced p. 68.

98 Tancredi and Clorinda II. 1953.
16″ high. Bronze, 1/1 owned by artist.
Reproduced p. 69.

99 Constellation I. 1953.
5″ high. Plaster, 1/1 owned by artist.
Bronze, 1/1 owned by artist.
Reproduced p. 70.

100 Constellation II (model). 1953.
5 3/4″ high. Plaster, 1/1 owned by artist.
Bronze, 1/1 collection Mr. Nelson
A. Rockefeller, New York.
Reproduced p. 70.

101 Acrobats. Study for a Monument
(model). 1953.
10″ high. Bronze, 1/2 collection Mr.
Louis Stern, New York;
2/2 collection Mr. and Mrs. Milton
K. Arenberg, Highland Park, Ill.
Slight variation in the two casts.
Reproduced p. 72.

1954

102 Study for Ballet. 1953/54.
18″ long. Bronze, 1/3 collection Mr. and
Mrs. E. J. Mathews, New York;
2/3 collection Mr. Robert D. Stecker,
Dallas, Texas; 3/3 owned by artist.
Slight variation in the three casts.
1/3 reproduced p. 74 top,
2/3 reproduced p. 74 bottom,
3/3 reproduced p. 75.

103 Ballet. 1954.
42″ long. Bronze, 1/8 collection
Mr. and Mrs. Willard Gidwitz, Highland
Park, Ill. Reproduced p. 76.

104 Detail of Ballet. 1954.
21″ long. Bronze, 1/1 collection
Mr. Carlo Frua de Angeli, Milan.

105 Study for Young Diana II. 1954.
5 1/8″ x 8″. Bronze, 1/1 collection
Mrs. Edgar Tobin, San Antonio, Texas.
Reproduced p. 56.

106 Portrait of Mrs. Marcus Bassevitch. 1954.
15″ high. Bronze, 1/1 collection
Mr. and Mrs. Marcus Bassevitch,
West Hartford, Conn. Stone,
1/1 owned by artist. Reproduced p. 62.

107 Portrait of Wallace K. Harrison. 1954.
14″ high. Granite, 1/1 collection Mr. and
Mrs. Wallace K. Harrison, New York.

Bronze, 1/1 collection Mr. and Mrs.
Wallace K. Harrison, New York.
Reproduced p. 63.

108 Study for Libellule. 1954.
3 1/2″ high. Bronze, 1/3 collection
Mr. Nelson A. Rockefeller, New York;
2/3 collection M. et Mme
Marcel Valsuari, Cannes; 3/3 owned
by artist. Slight variation in the
three casts. Reproduced p. 78.

109 Libellule. 1954.
54″ high. Steel, 1/1 owned by artist.
Reproduced p. 79.

110 Study for Raphael. 1954.
6 3/4″ glass, 4 1/4″ statue. Bronze,
1/12 collection Mrs. Simon Boosey,
New York; 2/12 collection
Mr. R. Werner, New York; 3/12 collection
Mrs. Etta Steinberg, New York;
4/12 collection Mr. and Mrs. Leigh
B. Block, Chicago; 5/12 collection Mr.
Leonard Jacobs, Washington, D. C.;
6/12 collection Mrs. Walter S. Heron,
Pittsburgh; 7/12 collection Mr. John Loeb,
New York; 8/12 private collection;
9/12 private collection; 10-12/12 owned
by artist. Reproduced p. 80.

111 Raphael. 1954.
2′ 4″ high. Bronze, 1/8 collection
Mr. and Mrs. Marcus Bassevitch,
West Hartford, Conn.; 2/8 owned by
artist. Reproduced p. 80.

112 Fish in Reeds II. 1954.
12″ x 9 1/2″. Bronze, 1/1 collection
Dr. J. Boivin, Paris. Reproduced p. 81.

113 The Fables of La Fontaine (model). 1954.
20″ long. Bronze, 1 + 2/2 owned
by artist. Slight variation in the two casts.
Reproduced p. 82.

114 The Fables of La Fontaine (1/4 scale). 1954.
2′ 5″ x 5′. Painted steel, 1/1 owned
by artist. Reproduced p. 83.

115 The Fables of La Fontaine. 1954.
9′ 7″ x 20′. Painted steel,
1/1 Public School No. 34, New York.
Architects Harrison and
Abramovitz, New York.
Reproduced p. 84.

116 Portrait of Benjamin Fairless. 1954.
24″ high. Basalt, 1/1 collection
525 William Penn Place Corporation,
Pittsburgh. Reproduced p. 86.

117 Portrait of Colin Mackenzie. 1954.
14″ high. Marble, 1/1 collection
Mr. Colin Mackenzie, Edinburgh.
Reproduced p. 87.

118 Acrobats. Study for a Monument. 1954.
3′ 6″ high. Bronze, 1/8 collection
Mrs. Donald McLennon, Chicago;
2/8 owned by artist.
Reproduced p. 72.

1955

119 Acrobats. Monument. 1955.
8′ high. Steel, 1/1 Wingate Public School,
Brooklyn. Architects Kelly & Grusen,
New York. Reproduced p. 73.

120 Portrait of Richard B. Mellon. 1955.
18″ high. Basalt, 1/1 collection
525 William Penn Place Corporation,
Pittsburgh. Reproduced p. 64.

121 Constellation II. 1955.
40″ x 44″. Painted aluminum, 1/1 owned
by artist. Reproduced p. 71.

122 The Boxers. 1955.
11 1/4″ x 6 1/2″. Bronze, 1/8 collection
Mr. and Mrs. Alexander Laughlin,
Locust Valley, N.Y.; 2/8 owned by artist.

123 The Tree. 1955.
16″ x 10″. Bronze, 1/1 owned by artist.

124 Dancers. 1955.
12 1/2″ x 2 1/2″. Bronze, 1/2 collection
Mr. and Mrs. John Cowles, Minneapolis;
2/2 collection Mrs. Charles E. Payson,
New York. Slight variation in the
two casts. Reproduced p. 90.

125 Seascape. Study for a Gate. 1955.
7 3/4″ x 17 1/2″. Bronze, 1/1 owned
by artist. Reproduced p. 90.

126 The Seven (model). 1955.
15″ high. Bronze, 1/1 collection
Mrs. Henry Hood Bassett, Miami Beach,
Florida. Reproduced p. 88.

1956

127 The Seven. 1956.
34″ x 39″. Bronze, 1/8 owned by artist.
Reproduced p. 89.

128 Sylvan Notions. 1956.
9 1/2″ x 7″. Bronze, 1/8 collection
M. Jean Arp, Meudon;
2/8 owned by artist.
Slight variation in the two casts.
Reproduced p. 91.

129 Bremen Town Musicians. 1956.
15″ x 7 1/2″. Bronze, 1/1 owned by artist.
Reproduced p. 94.

130 Frog. 1956.
15″ x 13 1/3″. Bronze, 1/2 collection
Mrs. Herbert Morris, Philadelphia;
2/2 owned by artist. Reproduced
p. 95 above.

131 Frog. 1956.
24″ x 18″. Painted steel, 1/1 collection
Mr. and Mrs. Coe Kerr, New York.
Reproduced p. 95 below right.

132 Frog. 1956.
4′ long. Painted steel, 1/1 Eastland
Shopping Center, Detroit. Architects
Victor Gruen Assoc., New York.
Reproduced p. 95 below left.

133 At Play. 1956.
1 1/2″ x 2 1/4″. Bronze, 1/2 collection
Miss Leila Whittler, New York;
2/2 owned by artist.

134 Mother and Child (model). 1956.
6″ x 7″. Bronze, 1/2 collection
Mr. and Mrs. Alexander Laughlin,
Locust Valley, N.Y.; 2/2 collection
Dr. Herbert I. Kayden, New York.
Slight variation in the two casts.
Reproduced p. 92.

1957

135 Mother and Child (1/4 scale). 1957.
26″ x 37″. Painted aluminum,
1/8 Commercial Investment Trust Financial
Corporation, New York.

136 Mother and Child. 1957.
8′ long. Bronze, 1/1 The Mary and
Alexander Laughlin Children's
Center, Sewickley, Penn.
Reproduced p. 93.

137 The Flirt (model). 1957.
4″ x 4″. Bronze, 1/2 collection
Mr. and Mrs. G. L. Callery,
Wilmington, Del.;
2/2 owned by artist. Slight variation
in the two casts. Reproduced p. 96.

138 The Flirt. 1957.
22″ x 17″. Bronze, 1/8 collection
Mr. Nathan R. Allen, New York;
2 + 3/8 owned by artist. Slight variation
in the three casts. Reproduced p. 97.

139 Tara. 1957.
10 1/2″ x 6 1/2″. Bronze, 1/8 collection
Mr. Lou Silver, New York;
2/8 collection Mr. Percy Vris, New York.
Reproduced p. 98.

140 Two Musicians. 1957.
10 1/4″ x 4″. Bronze, 1/1 collection
Publishers Printing Company, New York.
Reproduced p. 99.

141 The Secret. 1957.
10″ x 12″. Bronze, 1/1 owned
by artist.

142 The Maze No. 1. 1957.
10″ x 12″. Plaster, 1/1 owned by artist.
Bronze, 1/1 collection Mrs.
Frederick Rauh, Chicago.
Reproduced p. 100.

143 The Maze No. 2. 1957.
10″ x 12″. Bronze, 1/1 owned by artist.

144 The Maze No. 3. 1957.
10″ x 12″. Brass, 1/1 owned by
artist. Reproduced p. 100.

145 The Maze No. 4. 1957.
39″ high. Bronze, 1/1 owned by
artist. Reproduced p. 101.

146 Pirouette. 1957.
13 1/2″ x 7 1/2″. Bronze, 1/1 collection
Mr. Joseph Hirshhorn, New York.
Reproduced p. 102.

147 Joust. 1957.
34″ x 17″. Copper, steel and brass,
1/1 owned by artist.
Reproduced p. 103.

148 East Wind. 1957.
17″ x 12 1/2″. Bronze, 1/1 owned by
artist. Reproduced p. 104.

149 Composition with Tendrils (model). 1957.
16 1/2″ x 12″. Plaster, 1/1 owned
by artist. Bronze, 1/1 collection Mr.
and Mrs. Werner E. Juston, New York.
Reproduced p. 104.

150 Composition with Tendrils. 1957.
58″ x 40″. Painted steel and brass,
1/1 owned by artist.
Reproduced p. 105.

151 The Chase. 1957.
Dog 4″, birds 1 1/2″. Bronze,
1/1 owned by artist.
Reproduced p. 106.

152 The Finish Line. 1957.
10 1/2″ x 4 3/4″. Bronze, 1/1 owned by
artist. Reproduced p. 106.

153 Abstract Composition. 1957.
7 1/2″ x 7″. Bronze, 1/1 owned by artist.
Reproduced p. 108.

1958

154 Somersault I. 1958.
6 1/2″ high. Bronze, 1/1 owned
by artist.

155 Somersault II. 1958.
8″ x 10″. Bronze, 1/1 owned by artist.
Reproduced p. 107.

156 Personage in Rain. 1958.
9″ x 10 1/2″. Bronze, 1/1 owned by
artist. Reproduced p. 107.

157 Reclining Figure. 1958.
6 1/2″ x 10″. Bronze, 1/1 owned
by artist.

158 Fountain. 1958.
9 1/2′ high. Bronze, 1/1 collection
Mr. William Benton, Fairfield, Conn.

Sculpture commissioned for the
American Pavillon at the
Brussels International Exposition 1958.
Reproduced p. 109.

1959

159 Composition. 1959.
9″ x 8 1/2″ x 8″. Bronze, 1/1 owned
by artist. Reproduced p. 110.

160 Tree. 1959.
33″ x 24″ x 14 1/2″. Bronze, 1/1 owned
by artist. Reproduced p. 111.

161 Study for a Park Bench. 1959.
3 3/4″ x 6 1/2″ x 2″. Bronze, 1/1 owned
by artist. Reproduced p. 112.

162 Christmas Composition. 1959.
15″ x 12 3/4″ x 3 1/2″. Bronze, 1/1 owned
by artist. Reproduced p. 113.

1960

163 Composition 1. 1960.
8 3/4″ x 8 3/4″ x 6″. Steel and brass,
1/8 owned by artist. Reproduced p. 120.

164 Composition 2. 1960.
6 3/4″ x 6 1/2″ x 7″. Steel and brass,
1/8 collection Mr. Paulo Bettencourt,
Rio de Janeiro; 2/8 owned by artist.
Reproduced p. 121.

165 Composition 3. 1960.
10 3/4″ x 7″ x 11 1/4″. Steel and brass,
1/8 owned by artist. Reproduced p. 122.

166 Composition 4. 1960.
7 3/4″ x 10″ x 9 1/4″. Steel and brass,
1/8 owned by artist. Reproduced p. 123.

167 Composition 5. 1960.
7 3/4″ x 12 1/2″ x 10″. Steel and brass,
1/8 owned by artist. Reproduced p. 123.

168 Composition 6. 1960.
10″ x 8″ x 12 1/2″. Steel and brass,
1/8 owned by artist. Reproduced p. 124.

169 Composition 7. 1960.
8″ x 7 1/2″ x 7 3/4″. Steel and brass,
1/8 owned by artist. Reproduced p. 125.

170 Composition 8. 1960.
14″ x 9″ x 9″. Steel and brass,
1/8 owned by artist. Reproduced p. 126.

171 Composition 9. 1960.
9″ x 8 1/4″ x 2 3/4″. Steel and brass,
1/8 owned by artist. Reproduced p. 127.

172 Composition 10. 1960.
10″ x 13″ x 6 3/4″. Steel and brass,
1/8 owned by artist. Reproduced p. 127.

173 Composition 11. 1960.
6 3/4″ x 10″ x 9″. Steel and brass,
1/8 collection Mr. Paulo Bettencourt,
Rio de Janeiro; 2/8 owned by artist.
Reproduced p. 128.

174 Composition 12. 1960.
11″ x 14″ x 5″. Steel and brass,
1/8 owned by artist. Reproduced p. 129.

175 Composition 13. 1960.
10″ x 16″ x 8 3/4″. Brass, 1/8 owned
by artist. Reproduced p. 130.

176 Composition 14. 1960.
6 1/2″ x 10 1/4″ x 12″. Steel and brass,
1/8 owned by artist. Reproduced p. 131.

177 Composition 15. 1960.
8″ x 9 1/4″ x 5 1/4″. Brass, 1/8 owned
by artist. Reproduced p. 132.

178 Composition 16. 1960.
7 3/4″ x 11 1/2″ x 4″. Steel and brass,
1/8 owned by artist. Reproduced p. 132.

179 Composition 17. 1960.
9 1/4″ x 10″ x 9″. Brass, 1/8 owned
by artist. Reproduced p. 133.

180 Composition 18. 1960.
11 3/4″ x 11″ x 5″. Steel and brass,
1/8 owned by artist. Reproduced p. 134.

181 Composition 19. 1960.
7″ x 15″ x 9″. Steel and brass,
1/8 owned by artist. Reproduced p. 135.

182 Composition 20. 1960.
10 1/4″ x 16″ x 11″. Steel, 1/8 owned
by artist. Reproduced p. 136.

183 Composition 21. 1960.
8 1/2″ x 10″ x 7″. Steel and brass,
1/8 owned by artist.

184 Composition 22. 1960.
13 $1/2''$ x 9 $1/2''$ x 12 $1/2''$. Steel and
brass, 1/8 owned by artist.
Reproduced p. 137.

185 Composition 23. 1960.
14'' x 9'' x 12''. Steel and brass,
1/8 owned by artist.

186 Composition 24. 1960.
7'' x 12 $1/2''$ x 10 $1/2''$. Steel and
brass, 1/8 owned by artist.
Reproduced p. 138.

187 Composition 25. 1960.
7'' x 15'' x 5''. Steel and brass,
1/8 owned by artist. Reproduced p. 138.

188 Composition 26. 1960.
7 $1/2''$ x 6 $1/2''$ x 6''. Steel and brass,
1/8 owned by artist.
Reproduced p. 139.

189 Composition 27. 1960.
10'' x 9 $1/2''$ x 10 $1/2''$. Steel and brass,
1/8 owned by artist. Reproduced p. 140.

190 Composition 28. 1960.
10 $1/2''$ x 8'' x 9''. Steel and brass,
1/8 owned by artist.

191 Composition 29. 1960.
9 $1/2''$ x 8'' x 7''. Steel and brass,
1/8 owned by artist.
Reproduced p. 141.

1961

192 Composition 2. 1961.
27 $1/4''$ x 24'' x 32''. Steel and brass,
1/6 owned by artist.

193 Composition 7. 1961.
6' 8'' x 6' 3'' x 6' 8''. Steel and brass,
owned by artist.

194 Composition 19. 1961.
21 $1/4''$ x 47'' x 27''. Steel and brass,
1/6 owned by artist.

195 Composition 29. 1961.
36 $3/4''$ x 33'' x 29''. Steel and brass,
1/6 owned by artist.

Bibliography

by Bernard Karpel
Librarian, Museum of Modern Art, N.Y.

References in Books

1 Gertz, Ulrich, Plastik der Gegenwart. 2. ed. p. 180, 256 ill. Berlin, Rembrandt, 1953. *Enlarged edition includes English translation of text.*

2 Giedion-Welcker, Carola. Contemporary Sculpture. p. 212, 306 ill. New York, Wittenborn, 1955.
Also German edition: Verlag Gerd Hatje, Stuttgart. *Brief bibliography.* New edition in progress.

3 Gilbert, Dorothy B., ed. Who's Who in American Art. p. 72 New York, Bowker, 1956.

4 Hitchcock, Henry-Russell. The Miller Company Collection of Abstract Art: Painting Toward Architecture. p. 114-115 ill. New York, Duell, Sloan & Pearce, 1948.

5 Ramsden, E. H. Sculpture: Theme and Variations. p. 39 ill. London, Lund Humphries, 1953.

6 Ritchie, Andrew C. Sculpture of the Twentieth Century. p. 37, 220, 226 ill. New York, Museum of Modern Art [1952].

7 Seuphor, Michel. La sculpture de ce siècle. p. 109, 153, 189, 191, 194, 246, 247 ill. Neuchâtel, Griffon, 1959.
English edition: New York, Braziller, 1960.

8 Valentiner, William R. Origins of Modern Sculpture. p. 120 (ill.), 132-133 New York, Wittenborn, 1946.

9 Vollmer, Hans, ed. Allgemeines Lexikon der bildenden Künstler des XX. Jahrhunderts. v. 1, p, 374 Leipzig, Seemann, 1953. *Brief bibliography.*

Articles and Reviews

10 Ashton, Dore. Mary Callery. Art Digest 27:19 ill. Nov. 1, 1952. *Review of exhibit at the Valentin gallery.*

11 Bower, Anthony. Sculpture. Art in America 46 no. 4:53, 57 ill. Winter 1958-59.

12 Breuning, Margaret. Decorative diagonals. Art Digest 21:18 ill. May 15, 1947. *Review of exhibit at the Buchholz gallery.*

13 Breuning, Margaret. Rhythms by Callery. Art Digest 19:14 Oct. 15, 1944. *Review of exhibit at the Buchholz gallery.*

14 Broner, R. Eastland Shopping Center, Detroit. Art in America no. 1 : 44 ill. Spring 1958. *Illustrated by the artist's "Frog".*

15 Campbell, Lawrence. Mary Callery. Art News 54:54 June 1955. *Review of exhibit at the Valentin gallery.*

16 Candee, Marjorie D., ed. Mary Callery. Current Biography 16 no. 7:19 port July 1955.
Includes comment from the Wadsworth Atheneum Bulletin, Art Digest, Art News, New York Times, New Yorker.

17 Current Biography Yearbook. p. 97-98 New York, H. W. Wilson, 1956. *Incorporates no. 16 above.*

18 Coates, Robert M. [Mary Callery at the Valentin gallery]. New Yorker 31 no. 6: 74 Mar. 26, 1955.

19 Cunningham, C. C. & S., J. A. Loren MacIver and Mary Callery. Wadsworth Atheneum Bulletin ser. 2 no. 43:1-2 Nov. 1953. *On the acquisition of the "Eurydice".*

20 Frost, Rosamund. Amerikanische Plastik der Gegenwart. Die Schönen Künste (Vienna) no. 1 : 46 (ill), 48 1948.

21 Johnson, Una E. Contemporary American drawings. Perspectives USA no. 13 : 92, 96 d (ill) 1955.

22 Louchheim, Aline B. Spotlight on sculptresses: Callery, Hesketh, Orloff. Art News 46 : 24, 59 ill. May 1947. *Review of exhibit at Buchholz.*

23 Mary Callery. Art News 43 : 26 ill. Oct. 15, 1944. *Review of exhibit at Buchholz (unsigned).*

24 McBride, Henry. Anent Mary Callery. In: Mary Callery [exhibition catalog]. 6 p. New York, Curt Valentin, 1952.

25 Mellow, James R. Mary Callery. Arts (N. Y.) 32 : 55 ill. Oct. 1957. *Review of bronze exhibit at Knoedler.*

26 Munro, Eleanor. Explorations in form: a view of some recent American sculpture. Perspectives USA no. 16 : 160-172 1956. *Biographical note, p. 169; ill. p. 160 h.*

27 Porter, Fairfield. Mary Callery. Art News 51 : 47 ill. Nov. 1952. *Review of exhibit at Valentin.*

28 Porter, Fairfield. Mary Callery. Art News 56 : 19 ill. Oct. 1957. *Review of Knoedler exhibit.*

29 Reed, Judith K. Slenderized Callerys. Art Digest 24 : 16 ill. Apr. 1, 1950. *Review of Buchholz exhibit.*

30 Sawin, Martica. Mary Callery. Art Digest 29 : 18 ill. Apr. 1, 1955. *Review of exhibit at Curt Valentin.*

31 Seckler, Dorothy. This march of sculptors. Art News 49 : 28-29, 66-67 ill. Mar. 1950. *Also refers to Buchholz gallery exhibit.*

32 70 Sculptors. Life Magazine 26 : 114 June 20, 1949. *Illustrates 3rd sculpture international, Philadelphia.*

33 Tokens of art in city schools. Progressive Architecture 40 no. 4 : 149-150 ill. Apr. 1959.

34 Two exhibits of sculpture. Architectural Forum 81 : 202 ill. Nov. 1944. *Reviews Callery exhibit at the Buchholz.*

35 Stretched statues. Life (N.Y.) 33 no. 20: 143 ill. (port.) Nov. 17, 1952.

36 Washburn, G. B. International jury of award. Carnegie Magazine 32 : 304 port. Nov. 1958.

37 Watt, Alexander. Mary Callery. Studio 149 : 28 ill. Jan. 1955. *"Ideograms" at the Cahiers d'Art gallery.*

38 Zervos, Christian. Reflections on the sculpture of Mary Callery. In: Mary Callery [exhibition catalog]. N. Y., Buchholz Gallery, Curt Valentin, 1950. *"Excerpts from an article in Cahiers d'Art, translated by Dolly Chareau".*

Foreign Articles and Citations

39 Die abstrakten Künstler. Das Kunstwerk 4 no. 8-9 : 85 ill. 1950.

40 Gindertael, R. V. Mary Callery. Art d'Aujourd'hui no. 4 : 4 ill. Nov. 1949. *Review of Galerie Mai exhibit.*

41 Mary Callery - Nouvelles sculptures: 1943 -1945. Cahiers d'Art 20-21 : 303-306 1945-1946. *Four plates.*

42 Schwank, Friedrich. Malerei aus dem Geist der Musik. Zeitschrift für Kunst 4 no. 1 : 70-75 1950. *"Zur Gegenwartssituation moderner Malerei in Amerika ... Abb. 74 : Mary Callery - Bronzegitter".*

43 Zervos, Christian. Mary Callery (en son atelier). Cahiers d'Art 29 no. 1 : 119-120 ill. 1954.

44 Zervos, Christian. Réflexions sur les sculptures de Mary Callery. Cahiers d'Art 24 no. 2 : 304-311 8 ill. 1949. *Excerpts translated in Valentin Callery catalog (1950).*

Catalogs

45 Sculpture by Mary Callery, Oct. 9-28, 1944 (Buchholz Gallery, Curt Valentin, New York). *Biographical note; lists 17 works; 5 illustrations.*

46 Recent Work by American Sculptors, Feb. 6-24, 1945 (Buchholz Gallery, New York). No. 6 by Callery.

47 Sculpture by Mary Callery, Jan. 8-30, 1946 (Arts Club of Chicago). *Lists 11 works.*

48 Origins of Modern Sculpture. Mar. 30-May 1, 1946. (City Art Museum of St. Louis). No. 91 by Callery. Preface by W. R. Valentiner.

49 Carved in Stone, May 27-June 22, 1946. (Buchholz Gallery, Curt Valentin, New York). *No. 2 by Mary Callery.*

50 Mary Callery: recent sculpture, 1944-1947. (Buchholz Gallery, Curt Valentin, New York). *Exhibited Apr. 29-May 24, 1947; 16 works; 8 illustrations.*

51 Third Sculpture International, May 15-September 11, 1949 (Fairmount Park, Philadelphia). *No. 61 by Mary Callery.*

52 Mary Callery: Exposition de sculptures récentes, Oct. 18-Nov. 5, 1949. (Galerie Mai, Paris). *Lists 22 works (1947-49); 1 illustration.*

53 Sculpture, Sept. 26-Oct. 14, 1949. (Buchholz Gallery, Curt Valentin, New York). *No. 9 by Callery.*

54 Mary Callery, Mar. 4-Apr. 2, 1950. (Buchholz Gallery, Curt Valentin, New York). *Preface by Christian Zervos: Reflections on the sculpture of Mary Callery; lists 23 works; 10 illustrations.*

55 Mary Callery: Sculpture, Mar. 5-24, 1951. (Margaret Brown Gallery, Boston). *"Courtesy Buchholz Gallery". No catalog issued.*

56 Mary Callery, Oct. 21-Nov. 15, 1952. (Curt Valentin Gallery, New York). *Preface by Henry McBride: Anent Mary Callery; lists 22 works; 11 illustrations.*

57 Seventy-five Years of Sculpture, Nov. 1953. (Museum of Fine Arts, Houston). *No. 4 and 13 by Callery; 2 illustrations; biographical note.*

58 Sculpture of the Twentieth Century. (Philadelphia Museum of Art, 1952; Museum of Modern Art, New York and Art Institute of Chicago, 1953). *Preface by A. C. Ritchie. Callery: p. 24, 41 (illustrated).*

59 Mary Callery, Mar. 15-Apr. 9, 1955. (Curt Valentin Gallery, New York). *Preface by the artist: Notes on my sculpture; lists 25 works (1953-55); 13 illustrations.*

60 Mary Callery: Cinq de ses dernières sculptures, Oct. 7-21, 1954 (Galerie des Cahiers d'Art, Paris).

61 Exposition Internationale de Sculpture Moderne. (Musée Rodin, 1956), *Biographical note, no. 32 by Callery (illustrated).*

62 Figure in Contemporary Sculpture (Munson-Williams-Proctor Institute, Utica, N. Y., 1956). *No. 6 by Callery (illustrated); preface by H. K. Prior; also exhibited Rochester Memorial Art Gallery (Feb. 1956).*

63 Sculpture by Mary Callery, Oct. 7-26, 1957. (Knoedler & Co., New York). *No catalog issued. Reviewed in The Arts (N. Y.), Oct. 1957, p. 55, and Art News (N. Y.), Oct. 1957, p. 19.*

64 From Rodin to Lipchitz (Museum of Contemporary Arts, Dallas, 1958). *Two works by Callery; 1 illustration.*

65 The Sculpture Collection of Mr. and Mrs. Ted Weiner. Oct. 5-25, 1959 (Fort Worth Art Center, Texas). *Illustrates "The Young Diana".*

66 Mary Callery: Symbols, Mar. 28-Apr. 22, 1961 (M. Knoedler & Co. Inc., New York). *Preface by Christian Zervos; lists 40 works; 3 illustrations.*

Reproductions

67 Supplemental illustrations: *Art Digest* 26: 23 Nov. 1, 1951; *Art News* 51 : 16 Oct. 1952; *Art Quarterly* no. 1 : 72 1954, no. 3 : 304 1954; *Cincinnati Museum Bulletin* new ser. 2: cover July 1952; *Design* 47 : 6 Apr. 1946; *Interiors* 108 : 18 May 1949; *Print* 9 : 57 Mar. 1955; *Progressive Architecture* 31 : 17 Oct. 1950, 40 : 149 Apr. 1959; *St. Louis Museum Bulletin* 37 no. 2-3 : 11 1952; *San Francisco Museum of Art Bulletin* ser. 2, v. 1 no. 3-4: cover 1952; *Vogue* port. Apr. 15, 1945; *Yale Associates in Fine Arts Bulletin* no. 17 : 18 Jan. 1949.

Index of Photographers